Illustrated **BUYER'S ★ GUIDE™**

Classic
JAPANE
MOTORCYC

Ron Burton

MBI Publishing Company

First published in 2000 by MBI Publishing Company,
729 Prospect Avenue, PO Box 1, Osceola, WI 54020-0001 USA

MBI Publishing Company books are also available at discounts in bulk quantity
for industrial or sales-promotional use. For details write to Special Sales Manager
at Motorbooks International Wholesalers & Distributors, 729 Prospect Avenue,
Osceola, WI 54020-0001 USA.

Library of Congress Cataloging-in-Publication Data Available
ISBN 0-7603-0765-2

On the front cover: Although often referred to as "K0" models, original-series
Honda CB750s like this example owned by Paul Miller were officially
designated "CB750." The K0 designation refers to 121 bikes that bridge the
gap between the original CB750 and the CB750K1, introduced in September,
1970. No actual K0 models were officially imported into the United States.
Photo by Jeff Hackett

On the back cover: Main photo: Germany's Target Design based the prototype
for Suzuki's GS1000SZ Katana on a concept bike that used an MV Agusta
four-cylinder engine, making the Katana the first German-Italian-Japanese
joint venture since WWII.
Secondary photo: Honda's CB92R Benly was one of the first Japanese
motorcycles to become genuinely collectible. Today clean examples are highly
prized by collectors.

Designed by Bruce Leckie

Printed in the United States of America

Contents

Acknowledgments

As you can expect, I have many people to thank for their help with this book. Eric Nachbaur, a longtime friend and a fellow vintage Japanese motorcycle enthusiast, helped immensely with the research, looking up old magazine articles and offering his own insight and opinions along the way. Thanks to Ralph Walker for offering guidance when I first started to write this book, as well as sharing his vast knowledge of Lilacs and Marushos. Many thanks to Bob Ellis for assisting me in photographing his bikes, proofreading parts of the manuscript, and providing his own views and perspective on many of the motorcycles in this book. My appreciation to Rick Seto for arranging the photo shoot of his bikes on short notice on a cool February day in the Toronto area. Thanks to Troyce Walls for taking the time to photograph many of the motorcycles in his collection and for enhancing my knowledge of motorcycles over the years that I have known him. Tim McDowell for helping with the photographs of his bikes and his comments and opinions about several of the Honda models. Tom Leonard for bringing out his GT750 for me to photograph, Robin Markey for explaining the many details of a CB92 to me, and Stanley Lynde for the motorcycles he comes up with and for his enthusiasm for all motorcycles.

Thanks to Bill Silver, Joe Broussard, J. Braun, Don Smith, Tom Kolenko, John Sullivan, James Rozee, Jim Elliot, Greg Shortridge, Jay Horine, Jim Townsend, Ellis Holman, and all of the members of the Vintage Japanese Motorcycle Club for the education that I've received by being associated with such a great group of very knowledgeable people.

Thanks to the many people who provided photographs of their bikes for this book. Their individual names appear in the credits for each photograph.

I also want to thank Peter Terhorst of Honda, Mark Homchick and Mel Moore of Kawasaki, Mel Harris and Avery Innis of Suzuki, and Bob Starr of Yamaha for their help.

Special thanks to Lee Klancher of Motorbooks International for the opportunity to write this book and for his assistance along the way.

Thanks, too, to my family, Nate and Tim, my two teen-age sons, for their enthusiasm for motorcycles and their continual prodding to go dirt bike riding. Finally, my greatest thanks goes to my wife, Andrea, for her never-ending support while I wrote this book.

—*Ron Burton*

Introduction

This book covers the classic Japanese motorcycles sold in the United States from the late 1950s through the early 1990s. Because of the great diversity of models produced by the Japanese motorcycle manufacturers, only the models that were officially available in the U.S. market are covered.

The motorcycles that I have included are the classic models that have been sold in the United States since Japanese motorcycles became available in the late 1950s or, for some manufacturers, the early 1960s. Classics and significant models that are highly collectible had a major impact on the market, are technically interesting, or in some cases showed great potential and may have had a greater impact if circumstances or the timing had been different are included. I hope you enjoy the selection of motorcycles and can appreciate why certain models were included and others were not. Also, as interesting as they may be, I have not included any of the various obscure models and brands that were brought back to the United States by U.S. military personnel stationed in Japan.

For the models discussed in the text I have included ratings tables that cover six categories using a five-star rating system with five stars being the highest rating. Ratings are given for Collectibility, Passenger Accommodations, Reliability, Parts/Service Availability, Handling and Engine Performance. The most subjective of these categories is the collectibility rating. The collectibility ratings are based on my experience and the opinions of owners and collectors that I have talked with. As with all things that are subjective and a matter of opinion, you will undoubtedly find ratings that you agree with and those that you don't. Feel free to factor in your own experience and the opinions of your own personal authorities on the subject when making use of the ratings in this book.

In addition to the subjective nature of the collectibility of a particular motorcycle, the collectibility of some models changes over time. Collectibility of a particular motorcycle is made up of several factors, including rarity, technical features and innovations, historical significance, collector demand, and the number of motorcycles available. While most of these factors are constant, the last two can change and over time affect the collectibility of a particular model. Changes in collector demand and the number of motorcycles available are more likely, though, to affect some motorcycles more than others. Motorcycles like the Honda CB92 are established five-star collectibles for which the demand will not diminish and the number of motorcycles available will not change. On the other hand, the Honda CB350, which has only recently started to generate interest among collectors, may come to be regarded as more collectible or less collectible depending on future events. The demand for the CB350 will certainly continue to grow in the near future as more of the bikes are seen at shows, more articles appear about them in magazines and club newsletters, and their collectibility becomes more firmly established. As the demand grows, the number of CB350s available will most likely increase as more people become aware of its collectibility and pull them out of their basements, garages, and sheds and put them up for sale. Since the CB350 was originally a big seller, it is possible that the number of CB350s available may become larger than the number of collectors looking for them, and the demand and collectibility will then drop back off.

Collectibility

NA	1
Bridgestone BS90	2
Bridgestone BS350	3
Honda CB77	4
Honda CS76	5

Passenger Accommodations

Honda CT90	0
Honda C102	1
Bridgestone BS90	2
Honda CB500	3
Honda CB750	4
Honda Gold Wing	5

Reliability

Marusho ST	1
Kawasaki A7	2
Honda CB450K0	3
Honda CB750	4
Honda Gold Wing	5

Parts/Service Availability

Honda CS76	1
Bridgestone BS350	2
Kawasaki H1	3
Honda CB750	4
Honda Gold Wing	5

Handling

Suzuki MT50 Trailhopper	1
Suzuki T125 Stinger	2
Kawasaki H2 Mach III	3
Yamaha RD 350	4
Yamaha FZ 750	5

Engine Performance

Honda C102	1
Honda CB350	2
Honda CB750	3
Honda CBX	4
Honda CB1100F	5

When it comes to collectibility, there are also the bikes that do not yet have the track record to ensure their future collectibility. These are the bikes that are 10 to 15 years old. Typically, the demand for most motorcycles is very small when they are this age. They are too old to compete with the new motorcycles based on technical features and styling and they are too new to be in demand by collectors. I've identified a few of these that I think have the greatest potential for being future collectibles at the end of each chapter. It will be interesting 10 to 20 years from now to look back and see how accurate my predictions were.

The other rating subject to change is Parts/Service Availability. This is related to both the number of motorcycles available and the demand for the parts and service. If the demand for a particular model increases, then usually the parts and service availability will increase also, since there is an increase in the potential profit to be made. Eventually, when demand or price becomes high enough for hard-to-locate parts, reproduction parts will be made. Currently, reproduction parts are made for only a very few of the motorcycles that appear in this book. As the demand for—and the value of—collectible Japanese motorcycles increases, the availability of both new old stock (NOS) and reproduction parts will improve.

The other ratings, Passenger Accommodations, Reliability, Handling, and Engine Performance, are not likely to change and thus are stated in absolute terms. An example of this is the Engine Performance rating of a Honda CB450 when compared to a Suzuki XN-85 Turbo. The CB450 does not receive as high a rating for Engine Performance as the XN-85 even though the CB450 was, for a period of time in the late 1960s, the biggest, fastest Honda that you could buy. In absolute terms the XN-85 deserves and receives the higher rating for Engine Performance.

I hope you enjoy the book. If by chance while reading you come across any significant errors, misstatement of facts or situations where you feel that I have missed the mark, please contact me. I enjoy the feedback and welcome the opportunity to learn more about this fascinating subject.

—*Ron Burton*
ronbrooksburton@yahoo.com

Honda

MODELS COVERED

C100	CB160	CB400F
CB92	CB450	CBX
CS76 Dream Sport	Z50 Mini Trail	CX500TC
CA77 305 Dream	CB350	CX650T
CL72 250 Scrambler	CT70	VF1000R
CB77 Super Hawk	CB750	GB500
S90	CB500	RC30

Prior to starting the Honda Motor Corporation, Sochiro Honda had several jobs that prepared him for his later success as the world's largest motorcycle manufacturer.

In his youth, before World War II, he worked as an automobile mechanic, owned an automobile repair shop, and even raced cars for a few years. As often happens in racing, Sochiro Honda was involved in an accident that led to his decision to give the sport up. After he quit racing he started a company to manufacture piston rings. Knowing little

The Super Cub, the first of a very long, successful line of motorcycles for Honda. *American Honda Motor Company*

about piston rings, he initially failed in his efforts. After further study and resolution of the problems, however, he was ultimately able to make the company prosper and eventually sold it.

After World War II, Honda decided to enter the transportation business. In 1946, to get started in his new venture, Honda established the Honda Technical Research Institute in a 12-foot x 18-foot shed in Hamamatsu. The first products for the new company were motorized bicycles powered by surplus military engines. The motorized bicycles sold well and the supply of engines was quickly exhausted. In order to continue production, and to build on this accomplishment, Honda decided to design and produce his own engine. The design was finished quickly and in 1947 the new engine went into production. The engine was a success and allowed Honda to continue to build motorized bicycles, but now powering them with his own Honda engine. The pieces for Honda's future successes were starting to come together.

Business continued to prosper and in 1948 Sochiro Honda founded Honda Motor Corporation. The first major goal for the new corporation was to design and build a complete motorcycle. In 1949 this was accomplished with the production of the first Honda Dream, the Honda D type with its 98 cc two-stroke engine and two-speed transmission. The D-type was a good first step and the two-stroke engine was typical of Honda engines up to this point, but Honda decided that in order to continue to prosper, he would need a four-stroke engine. In 1951, with the future in mind, the first Honda four-stroke motorcycle was produced: the Honda E-type. The E-type engine was a single-cylinder four-stroke producing 5.5 horsepower. This use of a four-stroke engine was to play a significant role in Honda's success in the U.S. market during the 1960s, as his motorcycles became known for their quietness and dependability.

During the next few years, Honda introduced more new models and sales continued to increase. In 1958, the model that would become Honda's biggest seller was introduced, the Honda Super Cub. As success

continued, Honda looked for new outlets for its motorcycles and decided to enter the U.S. market. The first U.S. test of a Honda motorcycle appeared in the December 1958 issue of *Cycle* magazine. In 1959 American Honda Motor Co., Inc. was established, and Honda took its first step toward becoming a major influence in the U.S. motorcycle market. In 1959 Honda also enjoyed its first international racing success, placing sixth in the Isle of Man TT Race in the 125 cc class.

By the mid-1960s Honda was a leader in the world of motorcycles. Kawasaki, Suzuki, and Yamaha had also entered the U.S. market by this time, and the Japanese manufacturers were gaining ground on the once-dominant British manufacturers. By the mid-1970s the Japanese manufacturers were the leaders in motorcycle sales and the British motorcycle industry had crumbled, with only Triumph left, struggling to survive. Through much of this takeover, Honda was continuously a major engineering, manufacturing, and marketing force in the U.S. motorcycle market.

1959–1962, C100 Super Cub (50 cc)

Collectibility	★★★
Passenger Accommodations	★
Reliability	★★★★ 1/2
Parts/Service Availability	★★★★
Handling	★
Engine Performance	★

Engine	single cylinder, overhead valve, four-stroke
Bore & stroke	40x39 mm
Displacement	49 cc
Compression ratio	8.5:1
Bhp at rpm	4.5 at 9,500
Transmission	3 speed
Primary drive	gear
Clutch	multi disc, wet plate, automatic
Brakes: front	twin-leading-shoe drum
Brakes: rear	single-leading-shoe drum
Tire size: front	2.25x17
Tire size: rear	2.25x17
Fuel capacity	0.8 gal
Wheelbase	46.5 in.
Weight	143 lb
Seat height	n/a
Quarter-mile	n/a
Top Speed	45 mph (approximate)

The Honda Super Cub was one of the first motorcycles Honda imported into the United States. For many people, it is also one of the most memorable Hondas because of its simplicity of use and its interesting styling.

The Super Cub was somewhat unusual in that it was a cross between a motorcycle and a scooter. This gave it an appearance that was unlike any of the Triumphs or Harleys that were commonly seen on the street at that time. With its leg shields and under-the-seat gas tank it didn't look like a motorcycle, but its large wheel size kept it from being considered a scooter. Because of the frame design, the rider had to mount the Super Cub in an unusual way—by stepping through the bike rather than throwing a leg over it. This led to the Super Cub and other similarly styled motorcycles being nicknamed Step-thrus.

Another interesting feature of the Super Cub was its automatic clutch. In order to pull away from a stop, all you did was to step down on the heel portion of the shift pedal and then twist the throttle open. The clutch would automatically engage and the bike would start to move. When adequate speed had been reached, about 15 miles per hour, you closed the throttle and stepped down on the toe portion of the shifter once to shift into neutral, then a second time to shift into second and then opened the throttle again. Shifting to third was the same process, except that it only required one push of the shifter pedal. The process was far easier to master and less intimidating than those of the normal motorcycle clutches.

The engine in the Super Cub was a 50 cc single-cylinder, overhead valve four-stroke with a kick-starter. Although this size engine did not make for streaking acceleration or high top speed, it did make for a bike that was fun and easy to ride. Also, the small engine size was another factor in making the Super Cub less intimidating to the novice rider.

The Super Cub was the earliest version of the Step-thru 50 line carrying the Honda designation C100. An electric start version was added in 1960 and was designated the C102. In 1962 the Super Cub name was dropped and the model designation was changed to CA100, with the electric start model being the CA102. The later versions of the Step-thru 50 were available in the United States until 1970 and continue to this day to be available in other parts of the world. The CA100 and CA102 versions of the Step-thru 50 are also memorable because of their prominence in the "You meet the nicest people on a Honda" ad campaign conducted by Honda during the 1960s.

The Super Cub is a collectible motorcycle because it was one of the first Hondas brought into the United States and because of its significance to Honda and motorcycles in general. By the end of the 20th century, Honda had produced more than 30 million of these motorcycles, and the vehicle was responsible for introducing many people to motorcycling. The Honda Step-thru is not an expensive collectible, but it is a significant motorcycle that many vintage Japanese motorcycle collectors and particularly Honda collectors feel has to be in their collection.

The CA100T was the trail version of the CA100 with a large sprocket and no leg shields. The front fender on this bike is a non-Honda period accessory. *Troyce Walls*

The left side of a CA102 showing the very functional, fully enclosed chain guard. The ignition switch can be seen in the side cover. This was a common location for the ignition switch in early-1960s Hondas. *Roger Burns*

1959–1962, CB92 (125 cc)

Collectibility	★★★★★
Passenger Accommodations	★★
Reliability	★★★★ 1/2
Parts/Service Availability	★★
Handling	★★★
Engine Performance	★★

Engine	twin cylinder, overhead valve, four-stroke
Bore & stroke	44x41 mm
Displacement	124 cc
Compression ratio	10.0:1
Bhp at rpm	15 at 10,500
Transmission	4 speed
Primary drive	gear
Clutch	multi disc, wet plate
Brakes: front	twin-leading-shoe drum
Brakes: rear	single-leading-shoe drum
Tire size: front	2.50x18
Tire size: rear	2.75x18
Fuel capacity	2.8 gal
Wheelbase	49.6 in.
Weight	220 lb
Seat height	n/a
Quarter-mile	n/a
Top Speed	80.8 mph (claimed)

Robin Markey's beautifully restored, very desirable CB92 with the Honda racing kit seat, exhaust, and handlebars. This photo was taken at the annual White Rose Motorcycle Club's Vintage Japanese Motorcycle Show.

The CB92 was another member of Honda's 1959 model lineup. At 125 cc the CB92 was considerably smaller than the Dream Sport 300 but was nonetheless a very sporting bike. If the stock CB92 was not sporting enough for you, there were CB92 racing parts available from Honda to make it even more attractive.

The engine in the CB92 was a 124 cc overhead cam, twin-cylinder four-stroke. The engine was rated at 11.5 horsepower at 10,500 rpm. To have an engine in a production street bike in the late 1950s that was capable of engine speeds this high was phenomenal. This was the period when bikes like the 175 cc BSA Bantam made just under 7.5 horsepower at 4,750 rpm. Also an extreme rarity for the time, but common on most Hondas, was the CB92's electric starter. The CB92, as would be expected, also performed well. Honda claimed a top speed of just over 80 miles per hour.

The frame on the CB92 was made of welded steel stampings rather than the more

commonly used tubes. This style of frame was used on most Hondas until the introduction of the Hawk and the Super Hawk in 1961. The CB92 front forks were leading links with stamped steel covers over the front shock absorbers. The front brake was a twin-leading-shoe drum and the rear was a single-leading-shoe drum. The rear swingarm was again fabricated from welded steel stampings. Enhancing the racer image of the CB92 were front and rear magnesium hubs and a small windscreen attached to the top of the headlight.

Honda had many racing parts available for the CB92—engine parts such as high-compression pistons, camshaft, exhaust valve, spark plugs, ignition coil, carburetor jets, and a megaphone exhaust. There were also heavy-duty springs for the front and rear suspension and a countershaft sprocket to change the gearing. For the rider, there was a racing seat and different handlebars. These parts and the others that were available from Honda for the CB92 are now difficult to locate but add value to any CB92 that is fitted with them.

The CB92 is extremely collectible and one of the most highly valued of early Hondas. While not as commonly seen for sale as the Super Hawks, CB92s do come up from time to time. Parts for CB92s are like the bikes themselves—available, but often requiring a fair amount of searching to locate.

A rear view of the CB92R showing its nice lines and padded gas tank. *Gerry Kashuk*

A close-up of the CB92R controls showing the tachometer, windscreen, handlebars, and steering dampener knob. Note the fitting for lubricating the cables and the star-shaped cable adjusters. *Gerry Kashuk*

Another bike available in Honda's 1959 lineup was the CA95 Benly Touring, commonly known as the 150 Dream. The engine was similar to the CB92 but was a 154 cc OHC parallel twin with a single carburetor and a four-speed transmission. The CA95 is an interesting early Honda, although not as common as the 305 Dream. *American Honda Motor Company*

1959–1960, CS76 Dream Sport 300 (305 cc)

Collectibility	★★★★★
Passenger Accommodations	★★ 1/2
Reliability	★★★★
Parts/Service Availability	★
Handling	★★★
Engine Performance	★★★

Engine	twin cylinder, overhead cam, dry sump, four-stroke
Bore & stroke	60x54 mm
Displacement	305.4 cc
Compression ratio	9:1
Bhp at rpm	24 at 8,000
Transmission	4 speed
Primary drive	gear
Clutch	multi disc, wet plate
Brakes: front	single-leading-shoe drum
Brakes: rear	single-leading-shoe drum
Tire size: front	3.25-16
Tire size: rear	3.25-16
Fuel capacity	3.4 gal
Wheelbase	51 in.
Weight	315 lb (dry)
Seat height	n/a
Quarter-mile	n/a
Top Speed	91 mph (claimed)

The Dream Sport 300 was one of the first motorcycles brought into the United States by Honda, and reportedly fewer than 200 were imported in 1959. Prior to the Super Hawk, the CS76 and the very similar CSA76 were Honda's largest sport bikes. The engines in these bikes displaced 305 cc like the later 305 Dreams, Super Hawks, and Scramblers but are referred to as 300s rather than 305s.

The Dream Sport is a very interesting bike with several intriguing technical features. As with the later Dream and Super Hawk, the engine was a 305 cc overhead cam twin. Distinctly different from the later 305 engines was the lubrication system, a dry sump arrangement with the oil tank being under the right side cover. Ignition

The 1959 CS76 Dream Sport 300 with its high-level exhaust and Dream styling was one of the first Hondas imported to the United States. These bikes are seldom found in this condition.

A front view of a CS76 showing the square headlight, stamped steel handlebars, and turn signals.

The CS76 had several interesting technical features, including its rotary transmission and dry sump engine. This is a close-up of the distributor.

was through a cam-driven distributor with the distributor cover on the left side of the engine head. Transmission was a four-speed rotary. Also included was an electric starter, which over the coming years would become one of Honda's claims to fame. Like other early Hondas, the Dream Sport also had turn signals. Performance of the bike was comparable to the later 300 Dreams.

Stylistically, the Dream Sport was part Dream and part street scrambler (a type of bike of that era). The bike had a square headlight, square shocks, flared fenders, and an enclosed chain guard like the later Dreams. The Dream Sport's front suspension, although really a technical feature rather than pure styling, was leading link like the Dreams. Where the Dream Sport was distinctly different was its exhaust system. With one high level pipe on each side of the bike running up at a slight angle and ending just above the level of the taillight, it gave the bike a very distinct appearance. Not until recently with the MV Agusta F4 has a motorcycle exhaust system looked as good when seen from the rear as the Dream Sport exhaust did.

In addition to the 300 Dream Sports, there were also several other versions of the dry sump Dreams imported in 1959. The C76 and the CA76 looked very much like the later Dreams but with the early 300 dry sump engine. The C71 Dream Touring and CE71 Dream Sport again looked much like the later Dreams but have the early 250 cc dry sump engine. All of these bikes are rarely seen and are all quite collectible.

As for the 300 Dream Sports, I was told by a long-time Honda dealer that fewer than 200 were imported in 1959. Whatever the true total number imported, they are definitely a very rare bike. If you are fortunate enough to find a nice original Dream Sport or one that has been nicely restored, expect to pay three to five times as much as you would for a similar 305 Dream. If you find a Dream Sport missing a few parts and in need of restoration, be prepared to spend several years collecting the parts needed to do the restoration.

1960–1969, CA77 Dream (305 cc)

Collectibility	★★★ 1/2
Passenger Accommodations	★★★ 1/2
Reliability	★★★★
Parts/Service Availability	★★★ 1/2
Handling	★★
Engine Performance	★★

Engine	twin cylinder, overhead cam, four-stroke
Bore & stroke	60x54 mm
Displacement	305 cc
Compression ratio	8.2:1
Bhp at rpm	23 at 7,500
Transmission	4 speed
Primary drive	single row chain
Clutch	multi disc, wet plate
Brakes: front	twin-leading-shoe drum
Brakes: rear	single-leading-shoe drum
Tire size: front	3.25x16
Tire size: rear	3.25x16
Fuel capacity	3.1 gal
Wheelbase	51.6 in.
Weight	372 lb (dry)
Seat height	n/a
Quarter-mile	n/a
Top Speed	86 mph (claimed)

The 305 Dream styling was very angular. This CA77 shows the rectangular shocks, creased and flared fenders. This bike is very close to original except for the reproduction tires. New whitewall tires in the correct size, as originally fitted to the Dream, were available only in a ribbed tread pattern at the time this photo was taken.
Gerry Kashuk

The square headlight, leading link suspension, and highly coveted Dream plastic tank badges are seen here. The infamous Honda electric starter is attached to the front of the engine. *Troyce Walls*

The Dream was the touring model of Honda's 305 family and at 305 cc was one of the largest bikes in Honda's lineup until the introduction of the CB450 in 1965. While the Dream name had been used on other Hondas, the 305 Dream was the Honda Dream most remembered by U.S. motorcyclists.

The engine in the Dream was similar to the Super Hawk engine, being an overhead cam, parallel twin displacing 305 cc. There were differences, though, in keeping with the Dream's intended purpose. The main differences were that the Dream engine had a 360-degree crankshaft (i.e., the pistons rose and fell together but fired alternately) and a single carburetor. The Dream engine also produced only 23 horsepower compared to the Super Hawk's 28 horsepower. Like most Hondas, the Dream engine had an electric starter.

Similar to many of the smaller Hondas, the Dream's frame consisted of metal stampings welded together. The engine was bolted to the frame at the engine head and at the rear engine case, and like the Super Hawk had no front frame member to support the engine. The rear suspension was a swingarm with twin shocks and a fully enclosed chain. The front suspension was also similar to many of the smaller Hondas using a leading link arrangement.

The most unique aspect of the Dream was its appearance. The styling was done with very sharp creases, and many items that were round on most bikes were rectangular on the Dream. The rear shocks were rectangular and rectangular covers boxed in the leading link front suspension. The headlight was almost square and the fenders were creased in a manner that made them appear to be rectangular. To add to the Dream's unique appearance, the trailing edge of both the front and rear fenders was flared. The appearance was quite different from the Super Hawk, but very appealing in its own way.

The 305 Dreams are another example of the early desirable Hondas. While Dreams are valued at a little less than Super Hawks or 305 Scramblers, they are nevertheless a very appealing example of the early Hondas. Dreams, like the other 305s, can be found for sale on a regular basis, but finding a Dream in original condition or nicely restored will require more perseverance.

1962–1965, CL72 250 Scrambler (247 cc)

Collectibility	★★★★
Passenger Accommodations	★ 1/2
Reliability	★★★★
Parts/Service Availability	★★ 1/2
Handling	★★ 1/2
Engine Performance	★★

Engine	twin cylinder, overhead cam, four-stroke
Bore & stroke	54x54 mm
Displacement	247 cc
Compression ratio	9.5:1
Bhp at rpm	24 at 9,000
Transmission	4 speed
Primary drive	chain
Clutch	multi disc, wet plate
Brakes: front	twin-leading-shoe drum
Brakes: rear	single-leading-shoe drum
Tire size: front	3.00x19
Tire size: rear	3.50x19
Fuel capacity	2.8 gal
Wheelbase	52.4 in.
Weight	337 lb (dry)
Seat height	n/a
Quarter-mile	n/a
Top Speed	74.4 mph (claimed)

The CL72 250 Scrambler with its attractive staggered exhaust. The gas tank, side covers, and fenders were silver, and the frame, headlight shell, upper forks, and the fork legs were either red, blue, or black. *American Honda Motor Company*

Tim McDowell's 1965 CL77 305 Scrambler, showing the muffler on the 305 exhaust. This is the later, welded-on muffler compared to the earlier, slip-on muffler. A CL72 with its staggered pipes is in the background. That's Tim in front of the CL72 overseeing the situation.

The drive side of Tim's CL77 with slotted chain guard, ignition switch in the side cover, tool tube access in front of the side cover, and steering dampener on the front end.

The CL72 250 Scrambler was the first of Honda's Street Scramblers. Like the street scramblers that followed, the CL72 was basically a street bike with high-level exhaust pipes, a skid plate, and braced handlebars. The CL72 did have other differences, though, that gave it a character and look of its own quite different from the 250 Hawk.

The frame of the CL72 was different from the Hawk, Super Hawk, and most other Hondas. Rather than using the engine as a stressed member of the frame, the CL72 had a full cradle frame that the engine was bolted into. The frame was painted black, blue, or red and with the silver gas tank, side covers, and fenders, the CL72 looked distinctly different from other Hondas.

The engine in the CL72 was a 250 cc overhead cam twin Type I engine with a 180-degree crankshaft. As was typical for a Honda Type I engine, two carburetors took care of the intake, and the transmission was a four-speed. One aspect of the CL72 that deviated from the Honda norm was that there was no electric starter.

The CL72 exhaust was two high-level pipes that ran along the left side of the bike. The two pipes were covered with a slotted chrome heat shield to minimize the chance of leg burns. There was no muffler on the exhaust system, so the staggered ends of the two pipes were exposed. To temper the exhaust note a little, there were baffles installed in each of the pipes, but the owner often removed these looking for more horsepower or just for the sound. The exhaust note from the open exhaust was quite loud but added greatly to the character of the bike.

In 1965 the 305 Scrambler, the CL77, replaced the CL72. The CL77 was very much like the CL72 but with the larger 305 cc engine. The exhaust was also changed, with the two exhaust pipes coming together in a small removable muffler at the back of the bike. Removing the muffler exposed the staggered ends of the two pipes, greatly increasing the loudness of the exhaust. This muffler was later welded to one of the pipes and was not removable.

The CL72 and the later CL77 are both very collectible, ranking essentially equal to the Super Hawk in their popularity. Both models are regularly seen for sale, although the early CL72s are less common. Like the Super Hawks, the Scramblers also had plastic badges that are now quite valuable and difficult to find. Also like most early Hondas, the Scramblers went through running changes, rather than model-year changes, during their production run. Because of this, the restoration of a Scrambler requires considerable study to ensure that the parts are correct for the bike being restored. These detail differences affect the "correctness" of the bike and have a distinct effect on the bike's value.

One of the confusing things about early Hondas is the question of what year any given model was. Honda was not using annual model-year changes when the first bikes were imported to the United States in the late 1950s. Changes and improvements were made on a running basis with no holding back until the next year. When significant changes were made, the different models' variations were sometimes referred to as the early model and the late model. Because of this, it is sometimes difficult to determine a specific year of manufacture for some of the early Honda models. This does not hold true, though, for all of the early Hondas. Some of the bikes between 1959 and 1963, such as the CB92, did indicate their year of manufacture by the first digit in the serial number, such as 9 for 1959 and 0 for 1960, following the model designation. Other very early models, such as the CS76, indicated their year of manufacture by two digits, such as 59 for 1959, in the serial number following the model designation.

This system of running changes was used up until 1968, when the K numbering convention was introduced. Basically, the first version of a model was the K0 with subsequent model variations being assigned sequential K numbers: K1, K2, and so on. Typically, the K number changed with the model year but not always. For instance, the CB750K0 was made in 1969 and 1970 and the CB750K1 was made in 1970 and 1971. The CB750K2 was made in 1972 with the K number changing on an annual basis after that.

In September of 1973, with the start of the 1974 model year, Honda adopted an official model-year policy. Even so, the K number designations were used for model variation up through 1976.

1961–1968, CB77 Super Hawk (305 cc)

Collectibility	★★★★
Passenger Accommodations	★★
Reliability	★★★★
Parts/Service Availability	★★★ 1/2
Handling	★★ 1/2
Engine Performance	★★

Engine	twin cylinder, overhead valve, four-stroke
Bore & stroke	60x54 mm
Displacement	305 cc
Compression ratio	10:1
Bhp at rpm	28 at 9,000
Transmission	4 speed
Primary drive	single row chain
Clutch	multi disc, wet plate
Brakes: front	twin-leading-shoe drum
Brakes: rear	single-leading-shoe drum
Tire size: front	2.75-18
Tire size: rear	3.00-18
Fuel capacity	3.6 gal
Wheelbase	51 in.
Weight	351 lb
Seat height	30 in.
Quarter-mile	16.8 sec. at 83 mph*
Top Speed	104.6 mph*

Cycle World magazine test, May 1962

The Super Hawk is another of the popular 305 cc models that were very successful for Honda in the 1960s. While the Dream was the touring model of the 305, the Super Hawk was the sport model. Until the introduction of the CB450 in 1965, the Super Hawk, along with the 305 Scrambler, was the largest displacement Honda sport bike and Honda model offering the highest level of performance.

The Super Hawk engine had a single overhead cam and a 180-degree crankshaft. The 180-degree crankshaft resulted in an irregular firing pattern, which Honda claimed made for a smoother engine. (Both the 305 and 250 engines using the 180-degree crankshaft were designated Type I by Honda. The 360-degree engines were designated as Type II.) It certainly gave the Super Hawk an interesting sound. Maximum power was developed at 9,000 rpm. This high rpm range was not the norm for most bikes of the period, and it was quickly recognized as one of the virtues of Honda engines. These engines also gave the Super Hawk and many other Hondas performance rivaling many of the larger bikes on the market at that time.

The Super Hawk frame was a standard tube frame but was rather unconventional, having no front downtube. Instead, the engine was used as a stressed frame member with the main frame being bolted to

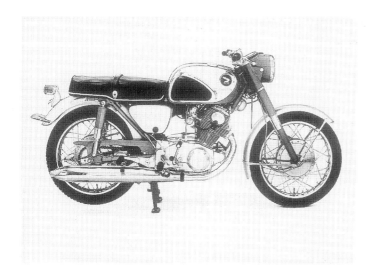

The CB77 305 Super Hawk was Honda's largest sport bike in the early 1960s. The CB77 paint scheme was similar to the Scrambler's with the frame, gas tank, forks, and headlight shell being red, blue or black with silver side covers and fenders. *American Honda Motor Company*

the engine head and to the rear of the engine cases. Brakes on the Super Hawk were standard fare for the time and were quite adequate even considering the Super Hawk's performance. A twin-leading-shoe brake was used in the front and a single-leading-shoe was set up on the rear.

Today, the Super Hawk is one of the most collected of vintage Japanese motorcycles. While not the rarest or most valuable, it is one of the most popular, and it can be found for sale on a regular basis. When purchasing a Super Hawk, be aware of the condition of the model-unique items, such as the exhaust and gas tank. Also be aware of the gas tank emblems. These should be made of plastic, have a wing on them, and say "300" at the bottom. These badges are very rare and can be worth anywhere from 10 to 50 percent of the bike's total value. If they're missing or have been replaced with the later, metal badges, the price of the bike should be adjusted downward by at least a couple hundred dollars.

A nicely restored white Super Hawk with the very desirable plastic tank badges. The paint scheme on white Super Hawks has been the topic of much discussion, since they are normally found with the common Super Hawk silver side covers and fenders. This one is finished with correct white side covers and fenders. *Roger Burns*

The Super Hawk, like the other 305s, also came in a 250 cc version—in this case, called the CB72 Hawk. Hawks were not sold in as large numbers in the U.S. market as the Super Hawks were, and they are not as commonly seen today due to their smaller displacement. This relative rarity does not make the Hawk more desirable than a Super Hawk, however. The larger displacement Super Hawk, even today, is still the preferred model.

1964–1969, S90 Super 90 (89 cc)

Collectibility	★★★
Passenger Accommodations	★
Reliability	★★★★
Parts/Service Availability	★★ 1/2
Handling	★★
Engine Performance	★

Engine	single cylinder, overhead cam, four-stroke
Bore & stroke	50x45.6 mm
Displacement	89.6 cc
Compression ratio	8.2:1
Bhp at rpm	8.0 at 9,500
Transmission	4 speed
Primary drive	gear
Clutch	multi disc, wet plate
Brakes: front	single-leading-shoe drum
Brakes: rear	single-leading-shoe drum
Tire size: front	2.50-18
Tire size: rear	2.50-18
Fuel capacity	1.8 gal
Wheelbase	47.1 in.
Weight	191 lb (dry)
Seat height	n/a
Quarter-mile	n/a
Top Speed	62 mph (claimed)

An S90 showing its slim gas tank with chrome side panels, rubber knee pads, and plastic tank badges. Although similar in design and material, S90 tank badges, as well as the tank badges for most of the other, smaller-displacement Hondas, are not as rare or as valuable as the 305 badges. *Roger Burns*

The S90 was another model introduced by Honda as it filled out its model line in the mid-1960s. The S90 also reinforced Honda's image as a maker of small, lightweight sporting motorcycles. A step up in displacement and performance from the Step-thru 50 or the S65, the S90 was a bike that a rider could move up to when the smaller bikes no longer had enough performance.

The engine is a single-cylinder overhead-cam, 90 cc four-stroke. Honda rather uncharacteristically supplied only a kick-starter on the S90 with no provisions for electric starting. The transmission was a four-speed with a heel and toe shift lever. Performance was brisk for a 90, with a top speed of over 60 miles per hour.

The frame was the common stamped-steel type used by Honda at the time. The front suspension was an improvement over the typical Honda leading link suspension with telescoping front forks with rubber gaiters. Handling and braking were both considered to be very good, bearing in mind the S90's size.

The cosmetic aspects of the S90 followed Honda styling for 1960s sport bikes, except for the long, slim gas tank. The gas tank did have the customary chrome side panels and plastic tank badges. The front and rear fenders were painted silver on the early models and chromed on the late models.

The S90, like many 1960s Hondas, is an appealing motorcycle. Almost everyone who rode motorcycles from the mid-1960s through the early 1970s rode an S90 at one time or another. The S90 is a reasonably priced collectible with a lot of appeal that can be found for sale on a fairly regular basis.

A view of the left side of an S90 showing the heel and toe shifter, stamped steel welded frame, and gaiters on the front forks. The canister above the engine contains the air filter. *Roger Burns*

1966–1969, CB160 (161 cc)

Collectibility	★★★ 1/2
Passenger Accommodations	★★ 1/2
Reliability	★★★★
Parts/Service Availability	★★★ 1/2
Handling	★★★
Engine Performance	★★

Engine	twin cylinder, overhead cam, four-stroke
Bore & stroke	50x41 mm
Displacement	161 cc
Compression ratio	8.5:1
Bhp at rpm	16.5 at 10,000
Transmission	4 speed
Primary drive	gear
Clutch	multi disc, wet plate
Brakes: front	twin-leading-shoe drum
Brakes: rear	single-leading-shoe drum
Tire size: front	2.50-18
Tire size: rear	2.75-18
Fuel capacity	2.5 gal
Wheelbase	51.0 in.
Weight	276 lb
Seat height	30.6 in.
Quarter-mile	18.6 sec at 69 mph*
Top Speed	85 mph (claimed)

Cycle World magazine test, May 1965

The CB160 filled the spot between the S90 and the Super Hawk in Honda's sporting line. Although not much larger in displacement than the S90, the CB160 was actually much closer to the Super Hawk in both specifications and appearance than it was to the S90.

The CB160 had a twin-cylinder, single overhead cam engine similar to that of the Super Hawk, only in a smaller package. Where the CB160 did differ was that the engine had a 360-degree

The CL90, a street scrambler version of the S90, was introduced in 1967. Typical street scrambler changes included the high-level exhaust, high handlebars, and shortened front fender. The gas tank is also different from the S90s and not nearly as attractive. *Roger Burns*

crankshaft rather than the 180-degree crankshaft found in the Super Hawk. Like the Super Hawk, though, the CB160 had dual carburetors, dual exhaust, and a four-speed transmission. The frame on the CB160 was also similar to the Super Hawk, with the engine being a stressed member of the frame and with no frame downtube running under the engine.

The CB 160's appearance was again similar to the Super Hawk's: chrome side panels on the tank, plastic tank badges, rubber tank knee pads, and silver side covers and fenders. One visual difference, though, was the cylindrical toolbox just below the side covers on the CB160. All together, the CB160 was very typical of mid-1960s Honda styling.

The CB160 was the sport bike that filled the spot in the Honda lineup between the S90 and the Super Hawk in the mid to late 1960s. The CB160 used the standard Honda paint scheme of the time with the frame, gas tank, forks, shocks, and headlight being black, red, blue, or white with silver side covers and fenders. The canister over the engine is the tool box. *Troyce Walls*

Performance was reasonable for the engine size, with the engine being typically Honda with a 10,000 rpm redline. Handling was considered to be very much to the standard of the time.

In 1966 the street scrambler version of the 160 was introduced. The differences between the CL160 and the CB160 were representative of street scramblers in the 1960s. The CL160 sported braced handlebars, a non-chrome gas tank, high-level exhaust, and no electric starter. For those that liked the street scrambler look, it was a very appealing bike.

The CB160 and the CL160 are both desirable bikes that are representative of the Honda styling and engine technology of the period. While not having the performance of the 305s, the CB160 and the CL160 are nonetheless appealing bikes to Honda collectors. CB160s appear for sale fairly often, and since they were manufactured for more years, are more often available than the CL160s.

The CB160 was also available as a street scrambler, the CL160, with its high handlebars and high-level exhaust. *American Honda Motor Company*

1965–1974, CB450 (444 cc)

Collectibility	★★★★ 1/2
Passenger Accommodations	★★★ 1/2
Reliability	★★★ 1/2
Parts/Service Availability	★★★
Handling	★★★
Engine Performance	★★ 1/2

Engine	twin cylinder, overhead cam, four-stroke
Bore & stroke	70x57.8 mm
Displacement	444 cc
Compression ratio	8.5:1
Bhp at rpm	43 at 8,500
Transmission	4 speed
Primary drive	spur gears
Clutch	multi disc, wet plate
Brakes: front	twin-leading-shoe drum
Brakes: rear	single-leading-shoe drum
Tire size: front	3.25x18
Tire size: rear	3.50x18
Fuel capacity	4.2 gal
Wheelbase	53.0 in.
Weight	425 lb
Seat height	31.5 in.
Quarter-mile	15.2 sec at 85 mph*
Top Speed	102 mph*

Cycle World magazine test, September 1965

Introduced in 1965, the CB450 was the successor to the Super Hawk as Honda's largest displacement performance motorcycle. While the Super Hawk was quite quick for its size and able to run with many of the British 650s, the CB450 pushed the performance envelope even further and reinforced Honda's reputation as a manufacturer of technically innovative and sophisticated motorcycles.

The engine in the CB450 included several technical innovations. The engine was a four-stroke, dual overhead cam twin with a 180-degree crankshaft. Up until the introduction of the CB450, the use of dual overhead cams was seldom seen on production street bikes. Also, interestingly, rather than valve springs the engine used torsion bars to close the valves. Another technical innovation was the carburetors, which were the constant velocity type, and although rather unique at the time, were to become common in later years.

The chassis of the CB450 was different than the Super Hawk and followed the common chassis design of the time with a full cradle frame. Brakes were twin leading-shoe drums at the front and single leading-shoe drums at the rear. Handling was considered to be very good in reference to the standard of the day.

To start, I like the look of the Black Bomber. While a lot of people did not like its appearance when the bike was new, I liked it from the first time I saw one in 1966. I never could understand why anyone would want to replace that gas tank.

The bike I'm riding is a nicely restored, although not perfect, 1966 CB450K0. The black paint and chrome side panels on the tank give the bike a very purposeful look. The silver fenders and side covers complete the very attractive Honda styling.

I sit on the bike and am immediately aware of its size. It's bigger than a Super Hawk but not as big as a CB750. It feels right, though. If you were accustomed to riding bikes newer than the CB450, you would quickly adapt. Everything is right where you would expect to find it, with the exception of the ignition switch. By the mid-1960s, the Honda ignition switch had migrated forward, from the side cover to just under the left front end of the gas tank, but it was still not readily accessible.

I turn on the fuel petcock under the right side of the gas tank and flip up the choke lever on the left carburetor, then feel around under the front of the tank and turn the ignition switch on. The green neutral light comes on, so I press the starter button. The starter cranks for a second then the engine fires and comes to life. I give it a little throttle to keep the engine running. After running for a short time the engine sputters a bit, so I reach down and flip the choke lever about halfway down. I don't push the lever all the way down yet, since it will need to run a few minutes before it won't require any choke. I give the bike the time it needs to warm up, push the choke lever all the way down, and I'm ready to go.

I put the bike in first, pull out onto the road and accelerate. The bike accelerates quickly, but certainly won't scare anyone who rides newer bikes in this displacement range. The feel and sound of the engine as the bike accelerates, while quite pleasant, is a definite reminder that you are riding a twin-cylinder motorcycle. I'm coming up behind a couple of cars so I roll off the

Desirability of the appearance of the CB450 depended on your taste. While the humpback look is today considered very appealing as typical 1960s Honda styling, this was not the case for everyone when the bike was new. Many magazines of the time ran ads for teardrop-shaped gas tanks to replace the CB450's hump-shaped stock tank.

The CB450K0s, so named after the K numbering convention started in 1968, were made from 1965 through 1968. The K0s, commonly referred to as the Black Bombers, with their four-speed transmission and humped-back tank, are the most desirable of the CB450s by a fairly large margin. CB450K0s appear from time to time, but very good to excellent models are hard to find. The K1s, with their more flowing tank shape and five-speed transmission, are the second most desirable of the 450s and are starting to gain favor with collectors, although they are the most difficult of the 450s to find. The K2s through the K7s, while being an improvement mechanically over the K0s, are not nearly as desirable as the earlier models. As such, they are much easier to find and are priced accordingly. The CB500T was the final version of the CB450 and is the least desirable of the line.

throttle and settle into the pace of the cars in front of me. The bike is comfortable and very pleasant for cruising along with the traffic.

After a few miles, the road turns twisty and the cars in front of me turn off, so I pick up the pace. From the way the bike handles, it's apparent that when this bike was restored, more than just the cosmetics were tended to. I get through the twisties and come to a section of the road that runs fairly straight for several miles. I pick a comfortable speed and check my speedometer; I'm doing a little under 70 miles per hour—certainly a respectable speed for covering distance on the more entertaining back roads. I guess my bias shows. I've always liked the Black Bomber since the first time I saw one. Going for this ride just reinforces my feelings.

This ride does remind me of an important point about buying a bike that someone else has restored. Don't be taken in by pretty paint and shiny chrome. Be sure that the same care was given to the bike's mechanical parts as was given to its cosmetics. There are few things worse than paying the price for a beautifully restored bike only to have the forks bottom out when you hit the first bump or have the transmission pop out of gear when you're showing your friends how fast your newly acquired prize possession is.

The CB450K0, Black Bomber, became Honda's largest displacement sport bike with its introduction in 1965. The humpback look of the gas tank was considered at the time to be unattractive by many. Now the hump is considered classic Honda styling. *Troyce Walls*

The CB450K1 with its revised gas tank styling, chrome fenders, and five-speed transmission was an improvement in many ways over the Black Bomber. The popularity of the K1 is increasing among collectors, but the Black Bomber is still the bike of choice. *Troyce Walls*

When the Black Bomber did not sell as well as expected, Honda came up with a kit to convert the bike to a street scrambler, hoping to increase sales. The conversion kit was installed by the dealers, giving us the street scrambler version of the Black Bomber, the CB450D. Although there were several parts to the kit, including gas tank and side cover emblems, the most noticeable was the exhaust. This differed from the later CL450s in that on the CB450D there was one high-level pipe on each side of the motorcycle. Later examples of the CB450D were also assembled at the factory. *Troyce Walls* .

1968–1998, Z50 (49 cc)

Collectibility	★★★★
Passenger Accommodations	1/2
Reliability	★★★★★
Parts/Service Availability	★★★ 1/2
Handling	★
Engine Performance	★

Engine	single cylinder, overhead cam, four-stroke
Bore & stroke	39x41.4 mm
Displacement	49 cc
Compression ratio	8.8:1
Bhp at rpm	1.95 at 5,000
Transmission	3 speed
Primary drive	gear
Clutch	multi disc, wet plate, automatic
Brakes: front	single-leading-shoe drum
Brakes: rear	single-leading-shoe drum
Tire size: front	3.50x8
Tire size: rear	3.50x8
Fuel capacity	0.7 gal
Wheelbase	34.7 in.
Weight	108 lb (dry)
Seat height	26 in.
Quarter-mile	n/a
Top Speed	25 mph*

Cycle World magazine test, December 1968

With its small tires, fold-down handlebars, three-speed transmission with an automatic clutch, and bulletproof engine, the Z50 was a great success for Honda. Z50s are now very popular with collectors, with the early models being the most desirable. This is a Z50AK1. *American Honda Motor Company*

The Z50 entered the market at a time when mini-bikes were very stylish, and new mini-bikes were constantly being introduced and many different manufacturers were making them. The Z50 turned out to be quite different from the other mini-bikes of the late 1960s, in that it remained in production, with the exception of the year 1990, from 1968 to 1998, giving it one of the longest production runs of Honda's many motorcycles. In 1999, the Z50 was finally replaced by the XR50R—a model that is still, obviously, very closely related to the Z50.

The engine in the Z50 was an overhead-cam 50 cc single that was virtually indestructible. The transmission was a three-speed with an automatic clutch, like a Honda Step-thru, making for easy riding for a beginner. Only a kick-starter was provided. Both the front and rear brakes were drum-actuated by levers on the handlebars. The lever to actuate the rear brake was on the left side, in the position that the clutch lever occupies on most motorcycles. In addition, a standard foot pedal also actuated the rear brake. Top speed for the Z50 was a little over 25 miles per hour.

Although few functional changes were made to the Z50 over its production run, one significant improvement occurred on the 1972 Z50K3 with the introduction of the twin-shock rear suspension. *American Honda Motor Company*

The Z50 front suspension was sprung forks with no dampening. On the early Z50s, the rear end had no suspension, with the rear axle bolt passing though a loop on the rear of the frame. Rear suspension featuring a standard motorcycle-type swingarm with twin shocks was added in 1972 on the K3 model. Tires were 3.50x8 knobbies mounted on two-piece rims. The two-piece rims could be unbolted and separated from each other to make for quicker tire changing. For easier storage in tight spots, the Z50's handlebars folded down.

As a total package, the Z50 was exactly what a mini-bike was supposed to be: small, light, indestructible two-wheeled transportation. A bike that was easy to use, unintimidating for kids and still a lot of fun for adults.

The Z50 is a bike that many people rode as their first bike and that most other enthusiasts have owned or ridden at some point. This familiarity, together with its long production run makes the Z50 a bike that is highly prized and very collectible. Prices run from next to nothing to three to four times what a new XR50R cost. The cheaper bikes tend to be owned by kids and tend to be well used, if not abused. The high price models are for original or correctly restored early-model Z50s, or bikes like the all-chrome 1986 Z50RD, in excellent condition. Honda Z50s are often seen for sale in the mainstream classifieds, as well as publications aimed at collectors. They usually get snatched up quickly, since they are not only collectible, but still make a good first bike for kids.

Over the course of the Z50's production, changes were made to the styling but the basic formula and the engine remained unchanged. This is a 1985 Z50R. *American Honda Motor Company*

1968–1973, CB350 (325 cc)

Collectibility	★★★ 1/2
Passenger Accommodations	★★★
Reliability	★★★★ 1/2
Parts/Service Availability	★★★ 1/2
Handling	★★★
Engine Performance	★★

Engine	twin cylinder, overhead cam, four-stroke
Bore & stroke	60.4x50.6 mm
Displacement	325 cc
Compression ratio	9.5:1
Bhp at rpm	36 at 10,500
Transmission	5 speed
Primary drive	gear
Clutch	multi disc, wet plate
Brakes: front	twin-leading-shoe drum
Brakes: rear	single-leading-shoe drum
Tire size: front	3.00-18
Tire size: rear	3.50-18
Fuel capacity	3.2 gal
Wheelbase	52 in.
Weight	353 lb
Seat height	n/a
Quarter-mile	13.8 sec (claimed)
Top Speed	106 mph (claimed)

In 1968, Honda introduced the successor to the very popular CB and CL77. The new CB and CL350 offered improved performance, many technical innovations, and new styling. They proved to be everything the 305s had been and more. They were immensely popular in the late 1960s and early 1970s.

The engine in the CB350 was a 325 cc parallel twin with a 180-degree crankshaft and a single overhead cam. Carburetion was by dual constant-velocity carburetors, very similar to the CB450 setup. A major improvement was a five-speed transmission rather than a four-speed as used on the CB77. The total package gave the CB350 very good performance, with a top speed of just over 100 miles per hour. In addition to the performance, the 350 engine proved to be the epitome of Honda reliability, able to withstand abuse and neglect and keep on running. The

Bob Ellis' CB350K0 shows the mix of old and new styling for 1968. The gas tank still had rubber knee pads as on the earlier bikes, but the chrome panels and the plastic tank badges were gone. The gas tank had more flowing lines and the paint scheme was now two-tone. The year 1968 was also the first year since about 1960 that most of Honda's street bikes had turn signals. *Owner Bob Ellis*

This CB350K2 shows more of the Honda styling evolution. By 1970 the tank rubber knee pads are gone and the side cover and headlight shell are the same color as the upper portion of the gas tank. With its highly dependable engine, good looks, and good performance, the CB350 was to prove very popular. *Owner Bob Ellis*

CB350 proved to be the perfect motorcycle for many young and inexperienced motorcyclists.

The suspension on the CB350 was standard fare for the time. Telescopic forks in the front and a twin shock swingarm in the rear. Brakes were twin-leading shoes at the front and single-leading-shoe at the rear. Handling was considered to be very good and appropriate for the size and class of the bike.

The CL350 was essentially the same as the CB350, sharing the same suspension, brakes, engine, and transmission but with the very popular street scrambler styling. The main differences for the CL350 were the high-level exhaust, braced handlebars, and rubber gaiters on the front forks. The CL350 did have a few drivetrain related differences, though, with lower transmission gearing and an engine producing 33 horsepower rather than the 36 horsepower produced by the CB350 engine. The power output difference between the two engines was attributed to the bikes' different exhaust systems.

The Honda 350 was almost the perfect motorcycle. It had very good performance and extraordinary reliability with good looks—a very fitting bike for any collection of motorcycles. The Honda CB350 and CL350 have yet to become as popular among collectors as the earlier CB77 and CL77. Recently, this has begun to change with the 350s beginning to generate more interest and attract more attention from the vintage Japanese motorcycle enthusiast. Also, while the 350s were originally sold in large numbers, they have not in the recent past appeared in the "For Sale" ads as often as the CB/CL77. With the gaining popularity of the 350s, this situation is sure to change. Many of the bikes now tucked away in garages and basements will be pulled out and put up for sale or tidied up for display or sale at vintage motorcycle meets.

A beautiful example of a 1968 CL350K0. The CB and CL350 continue to gain popularity with collectors and are becoming more common both at shows and at swap meets. *Owner Bob Ellis*

This is a close-up of the rear of the CL350K0, showing the two-into-one muffler and the Honda embossed heat shield. *Owner Bob Ellis*

1969–1994, CT70 Trail 70 (72 cc)

Collectibility	★★★ 1/2
Passenger Accommodations	★
Reliability	★★★★ 1/2
Parts/Service Availability	★★★
Handling	★
Engine Performance	★

Engine	single cylinder, overhead cam, four-stroke
Bore & stroke	47x41.4 mm
Displacement	72 cc
Compression ratio	8.8:1
Bhp at rpm	5.0 at 8,000
Transmission	3 speed
Primary drive	gear
Clutch	multi disc, wet plate, automatic
Brakes: front	single-leading-shoe drum
Brakes: rear	single-leading-shoe drum
Tire size: front	4.00x10
Tire size: rear	4.00x10
Fuel capacity	0.65 gal
Wheelbase	40.7 in.
Weight	143.3 lb
Seat height	28.5 in.
Quarter-mile	n/a
Top Speed	47 mph*

Cycle magazine test, January 1970

The CT70 was introduced in 1969 and had the Honda automatic clutch and three-speed transmission that was so inviting to novice riders. Bigger than a Z50, the CT70 was more suited to adults yet still small enough to be easily transported. *American Honda Motor Company*

The CT70 was less influenced by style over the years than the Z50 was, and it retained much of its original look. This is a 1982 CT70. *American Honda Motor Company*

The CT70H departed from the simplicity of the automatic clutch and was equipped with a manual clutch and a four-speed transmission. The CT70H was only made for two years. This is a 1970 CT70HK0. *American Honda Motor Company*

The CT70 had many of the same things going for it that the Z50 did. At the same time, being an overall bigger bike, the CT70 had some differences that made it better—or perhaps worse—than the Z50, depending on your perspective.

The engine in the CT70 was a 70 cc overhead-cam single, giving the CT70 more power than the Z50. The transmission was a three-speed with Honda's automatic clutch. The CT70 had the Z50 brake arrangement with both the front and rear brakes actuated by levers on the handlebars and the rear brake also actuated by a foot pedal. Tires on the CT70 were 4.00x10 with bolted together split rims. For easier storage there were also the fold-down handlebars.

The frame was welded-up stamped steel similar to the earlier Dream frames. The frame, in addition to the gas tank's being under the seat, gave the CT70 its unique appearance. In addition, the CT70 had lights and all other equipment required to be street legal With its overall bigger size, the CT70, although not able to carry a passenger, was also better suited to being ridden by adults than the Z50 was.

From 1970 to 1973, there was also a version of the CT70 called the CT70H. This was like the regular CT70, except that it had a manual clutch and a four-speed transmission. Having a shorter production run than the automatic clutch CT70, the CT70H is less common.

The CT70 is a popular and quite collectible bike for many of the same reasons as the Z50. Like the Z50, the CT70 enjoyed a long production run and was ridden by many people as their first bike. While not quite as popular as the Z50, the CT70 still has a strong following. Asking prices for CT70s vary considerably depending on the bike's condition and whether it is owned by a collector or a first-time rider. Again, like the Z50, CT70s are advertised for sale on a regular basis but tend to sell quickly since they are good first bikes as well as being collectible.

1969–1978, CB750 (736 cc)

Collectibility	★★★★ 1/2
Passenger Accommodations	★★★★
Reliability	★★★★
Parts/Service Availability	★★★★
Handling	★★★
Engine Performance	★★★

Engine	four cylinder, single overhead cam, four-stroke
Bore & stroke	61x63 mm
Displacement	736 cc
Compression ratio	9.0:1
Bhp at rpm	67 at 8,000
Transmission	5 speed
Primary drive	2 chains
Clutch	multi disc, wet plate
Brakes: front	single disc
Brakes: rear	single-leading-shoe drum
Tire size: front	3.25x19
Tire size: rear	4.00x18
Fuel capacity	4.8 gal
Wheelbase	57.2 in.
Weight	499 lb
Seat height	31.5 in.
Quarter-mile	13.38 sec at 100.11 mph*
Top Speed	123.24 mph*

Cycle World magazine test, August 1969

Bob Ellis' pair of 1969 CB750K0 "sandcast," showing both the left and right side, the four-pipe exhaust system, and the front disc brake. *Owner Bob Ellis*

When the CB750 came on the scene in 1969, its four-pipe exhaust and disc front brake were visual clues to its level of technical innovation and hinted at the bike's significance in determining the future of motorcycling. Anyone who saw a CB750 immediately knew that this was a major leap forward for motorcycles. Today, the visual impact of a CB750 has become more subdued with the passage of time and the series of similar motorcycles that followed it. But the CB750 remains very attractive and, to the knowledgeable vintage enthusiast, very inspiring.

The CB750 I'm riding is a 1970 K0 model. The bike is neither restored nor absolutely stock original, but rather has been used as a very nice, well-maintained rider. The gas tank and side covers have been recently repainted in the original Candy Blue Green, but the bike does show a few blemishes here and there. All in all, it's a nice, presentable bike for riding rather than taking to shows.

Starting the CB750 is very similar to starting a CB450. I turn on the fuel petcock under the right side of the gas tank and flip up the choke lever on the left carburetor, then feel around under the left front of the tank and turn the ignition switch on. The green neutral light comes on, I press the starter button, and the engine starts. Like the CB450, I push the choke lever about halfway down after the engine has idled for a short period of time and then let everything warm up for a few minutes. One thing that is noticeably different from the CB450, though, is the sound. Where the CB450 sounds rather lumpy and brutish, the CB750 sounds very smooth and sophisticated.

I get on the bike, put it in gear, and ride off down the street. The sensations from the bike are very nice: a smooth engine and a nice exhaust note. I immediately think back to my first encounter with a CB750. I was in high school at the time. A friend of mine that normally rode a Kawasaki 350 cc A7 showed up one day on a brand-new CB750. He asked if I wanted to go for a ride. I

The CB750 was one of the most significant motorcycles ever produced. It brought technical innovations to production street motorcycling that had previously been available only on race bikes. The CB750 proved beyond any doubt that the Japanese manufacturers, and Honda in particular, could produce a motorcycle that was faster and more reliable than anything the British manufacturers could produce. The CB750 pointed the way for the future of high-performance motorcycles and influenced the design of motorcycles for many years to come. It was truly a milestone motorcycle.

The dominant feature of the CB750 was its engine. The engine was a transversely mounted, inline, four-cylinder, four-stroke. Four-cylinder engines were not new to motorcycles. American manufacturers Henderson and Indian had previously built fours, and British manufacturer Ariel had built a square four, to name just a few. In the late 1960s, however, the only four-cylinder motorcycles available were racers or exotics like the MV Augusta. The CB750 made the four-cylinder engine available in a production motorcycle.

The four-cylinder CB750 engine had a chain-driven single overhead camshaft (SOHC) and four separate carburetors. Deviating from common Honda practice, the engine lubrication featured a dry sump arrangement with an oil tank under the right side cover. Electric starting, common on most Hondas, was used, although a kick-starter was retained for the rare instances when it was needed. The transmission was a five-speed, and final drive was by chain. The exhaust system had four separate pipes giving a separate exhaust for each cylinder. The four pipes and four separate mufflers were a big part, particularly when viewed from the rear, of what gave the CB750 its unique appearance. Performance was very good, with quarter-mile times in the low 13-second region and a top speed of over 120 miles per hour.

A left-side view of the 1969 CB750K0, showing the front disc brake setup, the slotted side covers, and the side cover badges unique to the K0. *Owner Bob Ellis*

Another feature of the CB750 that was not common at the time, except on race bikes, was the front disc brake. This was a single caliper setup with a solid stainless steel disc. The brake was hydraulically actuated with the master cylinder and fluid reservoir mounted on the right handlebar. The rear brake was more conventional, with a rod-actuated single-leading-shoe drum brake.

The chassis of the CB750 was a conventional arrangement with telescopic forks at the front and a swingarm with dual shocks at the rear. The bike was big and relatively heavy, but the overall handling was considered to be very good.

The CB750 was a very significant—and consequently a very desirable and collectible— motorcycle. All CB750s were good running reliable motorcycles in their day, but the collectibility and value of different years and versions varies considerably. The very earliest of the CB750 were produced with sandcast engine cases. These bikes are by far the most collectible of the CB750s. A "sandcast" is worth five to eight times as much as the later CB750s. The next most valuable CB750 is the diecast (non-sandcast engine cases) K0s that have many of the features of a sandcast but without the sandcast engine cases. These bikes are worth two to three times as much as the later CB750. After the K0s, the CB750s are fairly equal in value, although the earlier bikes are generally worth more than the later ones. Availability is related to value with the later CB750s being the most often seen for sale, the K0 being available less often, and the "sandcast" being quite rare.

immediately hopped on the back and away we went. My friend made the most of both the acceleration and the handling of the 750. I clearly remember the sound of the engine and the spectacular sensation of the pull of the bike as we accelerated coupled with the crunch of the footpegs as they touched the pavement through some of the faster corners. Definitely something that sticks in my memory.

I find that the CB750 is still a very nice bike. While it's not as fast as current 750s, the acceleration is still quick enough to keep me entertained. As I ride down a nice, winding section of road, I feel very comfortable on the bike. As usual, I maintain a brisk pace and find that I don't have to work hard to do it. The CB750 is big enough and has enough power to be comfortable and easily maintain the pace. On the other hand, it is light enough not to be a handful in the corners. Also since it is neither a cruiser nor a replica racer, the seating position places no special requirements on my body as far as positioning. This is what motorcycles were all about before they became niche-oriented and very specialized.

So the bottom line is that the CB750, 30 years after its debut, is still a nice motorcycle. Its level of technical development means that even today it is an appropriate choice for a motorcycle you could ride on a regular basis. An added benefit of riding a CB750 is the knowledge that you are riding one of the most significant motorcycles ever made.

The right side of the CB750K0 shows the oil tank cover at the top of the side cover, the upper exhaust pipe heat shield, and fork gaiters. The horn is mounted on the left on early CB750s, as can be seen here. *Owner Bob Ellis*

A view of the CB750K0 instruments. The speedometer contains the high beam and turn signal indicator lights, and the tachometer has the oil pressure and neutral indicator lights. The front disc brake master cylinder can be seen to the right of the tachometer. *Owner Bob Ellis*

This is about the only view that most people saw of the CB750 in 1969 and the first few years of the 1970s. Check out the 1969/1970 Florida license plate, a nice touch to a beautiful restoration. *Owner Bob Ellis*

A close-up of a CB750 sandcast engine showing the early unfinned oil filter cover. *Owner Bob Ellis*

In 1975 the CB750F0 was introduced. Like the CB400F the 750F had a factory four-into-one exhaust and was the Honda sport bike in the 750 class. Although performance was good, the CB750F was no match for bikes like the Kawasaki Z1. *American Honda Motor Company*

1971–1973, CB500 (495 cc)

Collectibility	★★★
Passenger Accommodations	★★★
Reliability	★★★★
Parts/Service Availability	★★★
Handling	★★★
Engine Performance	★★ 1/2

Engine	four cylinder, overhead cam, four-stroke
Bore & stroke	56.0x50.6 mm
Displacement	498 cc
Compression ratio	9.0:1
Bhp at rpm	50 at 9,000
Transmission	5 speed
Primary drive	chain
Clutch	multi disc, wet plate
Brakes: front	single disc
Brakes: rear	single-leading-shoe drum
Tire size: front	3.25x19
Tire size: rear	3.50x18
Fuel capacity	3.7 gal
Wheelbase	55.3 in.
Weight	449 lb
Seat height	30.0 in.
Quarter-mile	14.31 sec at 94.43 mph*
Top Speed	105 mph (est)*

*SOHC4 Web site, http://www.sohc4.org/

The 1971 CB500K0 offered the SOHC four-cylinder, four-stroke engine made famous by the CB750 in a smaller package. Included in the package were the four-pipe exhaust and the front disc brake. *American Honda Motor Company*

Introduced two years after the CB750, the CB500 did not make nearly the splash that the CB750 did when it was introduced, but then again, few bikes have. What the CB500 did do, though, was to bring many of the best traits of the CB750 to a 500 cc-class motorcycle. Being smaller, lighter, and less expensive than the CB750, the CB500 appealed to those riders who did not want to pay the CB750's price or did not want a bike as big or as heavy as the 750. Being a four-cylinder, four-stroke, it also appealed to people who wanted something more civilized than a fire-breather like the two-stroke Kawasaki 500 cc Mach III.

The CB500 had many of the technical features that the CB750 had. The engine was a SOHC four cylinder. There were four separate carburetors to feed the four cylinders and a five-speed transmission to transmit the power. The engine in the CB500 shared many aspects of the CB750 engine, but not its lubrication system. The CB500 had a wet sump engine rather than a dry sump setup like the CB750. The engine in the CB500 was very smooth, as would be expected from a four-cylinder engine, and overall performance was very good, with quarter-mile times in the low 14 seconds range.

The CB500 also shared the CB750's visual trait of four separate exhaust pipes, immediately identifying itself as a four-cylinder motorcycle. There was also a disc brake on the front that was a further visual indication of the technical sophistication of the CB500. It offered excellent braking.

The CB500 was available for three years and was superceded by the CB550 in 1974. The CB500 and CB550, with the transverse four-cylinder engine, are early examples of the trend to the Universal Japanese Motorcycle (UJM) that occurred after the CB750 came on the scene. While not as highly sought after by collectors and not appearing for sale as often the CB750s, they are nonetheless excellent examples of early 1970s leading-edge motorcycle technology.

In 1974 the CB500 was enlarged, giving us the CB550: the same basic package with more displacement and power. *American Honda Motor Company*

1975–1977, CB400F (408 cc)

Collectibility	★★★★
Passenger Accommodations	★★ 1/2
Reliability	★★★★
Parts/Service Availability	★★★ 1/2
Handling	★★★
Engine Performance	★★★

Engine	four cylinder, overhead cam, four-stroke
Bore & stroke	51x50 mm
Displacement	408.6 cc
Compression ratio	9.4:1
Bhp at rpm	37 at 8,500
Transmission	6 speed
Primary drive	chain
Clutch	multi disc, wet plate
Brakes: front	single disc
Brakes: rear	single-leading-shoe drum
Tire size: front	3.00x18
Tire size: rear	3.50x18
Fuel capacity	3.7 gal
Wheelbase	53.5 in.
Weight	375 lb (dry)
Seat height	n/a
Quarter-mile	14.6 sec at 85 mph*
Top Speed	102 mph*

* SOHC4 Web site, http://www.sohc4.org/

The CB400F was the successor to the CB350F as the smallest of the Honda SOHC fours. The 400F was sportier in appearance and character than its predecessor had been, and its bigger engine and sporty styling made it a different type of motorcycle than the 350F.

The engine in the CB400F was essentially the CB350F engine bored out from 47 to 51 millimeters for a displacement of 408 cc. With the larger engine displacement also came a six-speed transmission. Other than these changes, the CB400F was very much like its forerunner. Brakes were a single disc in the front and a drum in the rear. Weight was up two pounds over the weight of the CB350F, to 375 pounds. Straight-line performance for the CB400F was comparable to other bikes of this displacement at the time. The

The CB400F with its four-cylinder engine and straightforward styling is both a very attractive bike and a very pleasing bike to ride. This is a 1975 CB400F belonging to Steve and Jon Paswater.

The styling of the CB400F's exhaust system makes it one of the best looking exhaust systems seen on a production motorcycle.

The 1973 CB350F0 with its four-cylinder engine was similar to the later CB400F but not as successful. While the CB350F is a desirable bike as a collectible, it does not attract as much attention as the CB400F does. *American Honda Motor Company*

best thing about the CB400F was that it did everything very well. The bike handled well and the engine had a feeling of "correctness" to it that is very hard to describe.

The styling of the CB400F was Honda's version of a café racer. With low handlebars, raised footpegs and a very simple paint scheme, the bike looked the part. The most impressive piece of the CB400F's styling was its exhaust system. This was a beautiful four-into-one exhaust system with the most visually appealing set of head pipes seen on any motorcycle. As an added benefit, the exhaust sounded great when the bike was accelerating hard and the engine was nearing its maximum revs.

The differences between the CB350F and the CB400F are interesting. While they are similar bikes in that they both have four-cylinder engines and were close in displacement to each other, the two bikes are quite different from each other in styling and character. These variations have resulted in a large difference in their collectibility. While the CB350F is a nice bike, the CB400F is highly sought after by collectors. The result of this is that CB400Fs are worth two to three times as much as CB350Fs.

The CB400F was produced for three years, 1975 through 1977. Being very popular bikes with collectors, CB400Fs appear in classified ads regularly. All three years are collectible, but the 1977 models do have higher handlebars, striping on the gas tank, and are slightly less sought after. The exhaust system makes up a large part of the bike's appeal and value, and should be given thorough scrutiny when buying a CB400F.

1975–79, Gold Wing (999 cc, 1,085 cc, 1,182 cc, 1,520 cc)

Collectibility	★★★
Passenger Accommodations	★★★★★
Reliability	★★★★★
Parts/Service Availability	★★★★
Handling	★★★
Engine Performance	★★★

Engine	flat four cylinder, overhead cam, four-stroke
Bore & stroke	72x61.4 mm
Displacement	999 cc
Compression ratio	9.2:1
Bhp at rpm	80 at 7,500
Transmission	5 speed, shaft final drive
Primary drive	chain
Clutch	multi disc, wet plate
Brakes: front	twin disc
Brakes: rear	single disc
Tire size: front	3.50H19
Tire size: rear	4.50H17
Fuel capacity	5.0 gal
Wheelbase	60.9 in.
Weight	584 lb (dry)
Seat height	32 in.
Quarter-mile	12.92 sec at 105.5 mph (claimed)
Top Speed	122 mph (claimed)

By the mid-1970s, the excitement over the CB750 had died down, and motorcycle technology had continued to develop. Honda's competitors were all hard at work with new and innovative bikes being introduced and many more in the works. Kawasaki had introduced the Z1, BMW had sported up the boxer twin to produce the R90S, and Suzuki had the two-stroke, water-cooled GT750 and was developing the rotary-engine RE5, to name just a few. As wonderful as the CB750 had been, Honda needed a new motorcycle to reestablish its image as a designer and manufacturer of cutting-edge motorcycles.

The first thoughts for Honda had been to develop a large, impressive motorcycle that was both a sport bike and a touring bike. With this concept in mind, a prototype with a 1500 cc flat six engine was built and tested. After further consideration, it was decided that the best approach was to let the CB750F assume the role as Honda's sport bike and to concentrate on building the ultimate touring bike. This new motorcycle would have to meet the touring needs of Honda's largest market, the United States, and would have to outperform and outsell all competitors. From these lofty goals the Gold Wing was developed.

The GL1000 Gold Wing was introduced in 1975. The early Gold Wings, although aimed at the touring market, had no fairing or bags; this was up to the individual owner to add according to his taste. *American Honda Motor Company*

Realizing the market for a fully outfitted touring bike straight from the factory, Honda developed several variations and trim levels for the Gold Wing. Full touring fairing, saddlebags, a trunk, stereo system, CB, and many other options were offered. Over the years the Gold Wing's engine got progressively larger, going from the original 1,000 cc engine to 1,100 cc, to 1,200 cc and then to the 1,500 cc flat six. This is a 1985 GL1200 Aspencade. *American Honda Motor Company*

The Gold Wing was a combination of new ideas and tried and proven technology. The engine was a 1000 cc flat four with belt-driven overhead cams. It was liquid-cooled, with a five-speed transmission and shaft final drive. The engine was very complicated, but also proved to be extremely reliable. The gas tank was under the seat and the container that occupied the space and looked like a regular gas tank actually contained part of the electrical system and storage space. The Gold Wing was heavy, weighing over 600 pounds when fueled and ready to ride. For its large size and weight, its handling, while not in the sports bike league, was still quite competent. Between the smoothness of its engine, its high level of reliability, and its ability to carry large loads with ease, the Gold Wing was very close to the perfect motorcycle for touring.

For the first few years, the Gold Wing was sold without any special equipment for touring. The owners who bought Gold Wings customized the bike to their liking by adding a fairing, bags, a plusher seat, a radio, or other items that the owner judged necessary to make long-distance travel more comfortable. Realizing the market potential of factory-built, fully optioned touring bikes, Honda eventually introduced models that included factory-installed fairings, bags, and many other accessories. This concept was developed into the Gold Wing Interstate, Aspencade, and SE models. Over time, there was also an increase in engine displacement and eventually the introduction of a flat six-cylinder engine.

The Gold Wing is a motorcycle that has a large following. Many people riding them would never really consider riding any other motorcycle. There is no doubt that the Gold Wing is a historical motorcycle and a bike with great appeal. Although seen for sale on a fairly regular basis, Gold Wings are not that common among collectors. They do show up at vintage motorcycle shows from time to time, but in nowhere near the numbers that CB750s or Kawasaki H1s do. This is perhaps in part due to the Gold Wing being such a commercial success and the fact that it is still in production. In time, the collectibility of the Gold Wing will undoubtedly improve. The early Gold Wings are the most desirable. While high mileage is not as important in determining the value of a Gold Wing, overall condition is.

1979–1982, CBX (1,047 cc)

Collectibility ★★★★ 1/2
Passenger Accommodations ★★★★
Reliability ★★★★
Parts/Service Availability ★★★★
Handling ★★★ 1/2
Engine Performance ★★★★

Engine	six cylinder, dual overhead cam, four-stroke
Bore & stroke	64.5x53.4 mm
Displacement	1047 cc
Compression ratio	9.3:1
Bhp at rpm	103 at 9,000 (claimed)
Transmission	5 speed
Primary drive	Hi-Vo chain
Clutch	multi disc, wet plate
Brakes: front	dual discs
Brakes: rear	single disc
Tire size: front	3.50H19
Tire size: rear	4.25H18
Fuel capacity	5.28 gal
Wheelbase	58.86 in.
Weight	599.9 lb
Seat height	31.9 in.
Quarter-mile	11.552 sec at 117.49 mph*
Top Speed	136 mph*

*Cycle magazine test, February 1978

The 1970s were not as exciting for Honda as the 1960s had been. Yes, there were some very interesting motorcycles like the CB400F, and some not only interesting, but extremely significant motorcycles like the Gold Wing, but there was not the excitement that there had been in the 1960s. During the time period that Kawasaki had introduced the Z1 and Suzuki had introduced and retired the GT750 and then introduced a whole new four-stroke engine family with the GS750 and GS1000, Honda was still getting by with the CB750 as its sport bike. While the CB750 was definitely a milestone motorcycle, by the late 1970s it was time for Honda to find a replacement for it.

The bike that Honda introduced as its top-of-the-line sport bike in 1979 was the CBX. The CBX, like all motorcycles, had many interesting technical features, but the one thing that dominated all other aspects of

The first year for the CBX, Honda's fast, smooth, six-cylinder technological marvel was 1979. *American Honda Motor Company*

The appearance of the 1980 CBX was very similar to that of the 1979, except that the Comstar wheels were black, and black paint was available in lieu of silver, with red being available for both years. The exhaust is an aftermarket Supertrapp system. *Author's collection*

In 1981 Honda changed the CBX into a Sport Tourer. A full fairing and detachable saddlebags were added, the rear suspension was upgraded to Honda's Pro-Link arrangement, and the front disc was ventilated. The color for 1981 was what Honda called Magnum Silver Metallic. *American Honda Motor Company*

this motorcycle was its engine. The CBX engine was a 1047 cc, transversely mounted, inline, six-cylinder four-stroke with 24 valves and dual overhead cams. Six individual CV carburetors, fed by a large air box, handled the intake, and the exhaust was a six-into-two system that sounded spectacular. The transmission was a five-speed with chain drive to the rear wheel. Honda claimed power output of 103 horsepower for the six. With a quarter-mile time of 11.552 seconds, the straight-line performance of the 1979 CBX made it the quickest production motorcycle made at the time.

To keep the CBX engine as narrow as possible, the alternator and the ignition-timing rotor were positioned behind the crankshaft rather than on the crankshaft ends. Drive for the alternator and ignition-timing rotor was by a jackshaft that was chain driven by the crankshaft. Overall width of the CBX engine was only 2 inches wider than the CB750 engine, but since the cylinders run almost the full width of the engine, the engine appeared to be considerably bigger and wider than the CB750.

The suspension on the 1979 and 1980 CBX featured the regular telescopic front forks and twin shock swingarm in the rear. Handling was considered reasonably good for the time, but care and forethought had to be given to the size and weight of the bike. Weighing just a hair shy of 600 pounds, the CBX was not a bike that was receptive to major line changes mid-corner.

In 1981, Honda decided to change the CBX's image to improve sales. A fairing and detachable saddlebags were standard equipment on both the 1981 and 1982 CBX. The idea was to market the CBX as a Sport Tourer. Other changes included chrome engine guards, the Honda Pro-Link single-shock rear suspension, twin-piston calipers for both the front and rear brakes, and an enlarged gas tank. These changes made the CBX one of the few bikes that came in two distinctly different versions during its production run. In the end, the changes were not enough to boost the sales to the level that Honda wanted, and 1982 was the last year for the CBX.

The CBX, whether it's an unfaired 1979 or 1980 or the Sport Touring 1981 or 1982, is a collectible motorcycle. The most desirable members of the group are the first year 1979 models—even though 1979 was the year that the largest number of CBXs were produced. Availability is good for all years, so don't be impatient and grab the first CBX that becomes available. When buying a CBX, review the seller's records to be sure that the engine has been properly maintained and is in good running order. While this is good advice when buying any motorcycle, I stress this point about the CBX because of the complexity of the engine. Also be sure that the carburetors are clean and working properly, since removing them for cleaning requires that the exhaust system be removed and the engine unbolted from the frame and tilted forward. Add the time to do this to the time required to clean six carburetors and you can appreciate the significance of this point. In the end, patience will pay off and your search will be worth the time, since a good-running CBX is one of the nicest motorcycles that Honda has ever produced.

1982, CX500 TC (497 cc)

Collectibility	★★★★
Passenger Accommodations	★★★
Reliability	★★★ 1/2
Parts/Service Availability	★★★
Handling	★★★
Engine Performance	★★★★

Engine	twin cylinder, overhead valve, turbo-charged four-stroke
Bore & stroke	78x52 mm
Displacement	497 cc
Compression ratio	7.2:1
Bhp at rpm	n/a
Transmission	5 speed
Primary drive	straight cut gear
Clutch	multi disc, wet plate
Brakes: front	twin disc, dual piston caliper
Brakes: rear	single disc, dual piston caliper
Tire size: front	3.50V19
Tire size: rear	120/90-17
Fuel capacity	5.3 gal
Wheelbase	58.9 in.
Weight	578 lb
Seat height	31.3 in.
Quarter-mile	12.38 sec at 106 mph*
Top Speed	120 mph*

Cycle magazine test, July 1982

The 1982 CX500TC was a technological phenomenon. With its elaborate monitoring and control systems, turbocharger and advanced suspension, the CX500TC showed off both Honda's engineering and manufacturing capabilities. *American Honda Motor Company*

Turbocharging

Prior to the overabundance of turbocharged vehicles in the 1980s, turbocharging had been successfully used in racing cars and airplanes. In the early 1980s, turbocharging became increasingly popular, and many of the major automobile manufacturers developed and marketed turbocharged cars. During this time, turbocharging became so pervasive that the word turbo was applied to many things that had nothing to do with internal combustion engines. Before it all ended, there was Turbo cologne and nearly every computer made had a turbo button on it that made the computer run faster. To incorporate the popular culture and ensure that they benefited from the technological promise, the Japanese motorcycle manufacturers also got swept into the frenzy.

The idea of turbocharging was fairly straightforward. By turbocharging the engine, more power could be produced for a given displacement. The turbocharger assembly, together with the smaller displacement engine, would weigh less than a larger displacement engine making the same amount of power. The idea seemed to be the future of performance vehicles of all types, including motorcycles. In the end, turbocharging was not the panacea for motorcycles that everyone had thought it would be. Honda, Kawasaki, Suzuki, and Yamaha all built turbocharged motorcycles for only a very few years. The complexity, problems associated with turbocharging, and poor sales brought an end to the era of turbocharged motorcycles. From that short period of time, we have a handful of very technologically interesting collectible motorcycles.

Honda, like the other Japanese motorcycle manufacturers, took the plunge in the early 1980s and built turbocharged motorcycles. Honda led the way in this technological dead end with the first factory-produced turbo, the CX500TC. Like the other manufacturers, though, it did not take Honda long to determine that turbocharging was not well suited for use on motorcycles.

The CX500 Turbo was a complete factory-developed turbocharged motorcycle. As the engine for the project Honda chose its CX500 longitudinally mounted v-twin engine, which had been developed with turbocharging in mind. Honda then spent time and money making sure that its Turbo was not only fast, but also reliable and capable of functioning properly under all the conditions its owners were likely to expose it to. As is often the case with cutting-edge Honda motorcycles, the CX500 Turbo was also a statement about Honda's engineering capabilities.

Honda worked with IHI (Ishikawajima-Harima Industries), the turbocharger manufacturer, to develop a turbocharger specifically for the CX500TC. At the time, the CX500TC turbocharger was the smallest turbocharger made, and it ran at an operating speed of 180,000 rpm. The complete induction system for the CX500TC was very complex. In addition to the turbocharger there was a resonance chamber, a surge tank, a reed valve, an air valve, and a throttle valve in the intake. There were also sensors to monitor throttle position, engine speed, coolant temperature, atmospheric pressure, air temperature, and manifold pressure. To oversee all of the sensors in the system and control the fuel injectors, Honda developed a digital computer control system dubbed CFI (computerized fuel injection). In addition to the CFI, there was also a separate computer that sensed boost pressure and engine speed, and controlled the ignition timing. This complicated system, monitoring and controlling the many variables associated with a turbocharged motorcycle engine, allowed the CX500TC to start developing boost at about 3,500 rpm and limited maximum boost pressure to 17.4 psi. All of this added up to a very fast but an extremely complex 500 cc motorcycle.

The chassis of the CX500TC was also quite sophisticated. The front suspension sported 37-millimeter fork tubes (large diameter fork tubes for a 500 at the time) and Honda's TRAC anti-dive forks. The rear end had a box section aluminum swingarm and Honda's single shock Pro-link suspension. The handling of the CX500TC was fairly reasonable, but the bike was heavy and steering response was slower than the pure sport bikes of the day. In addition to the basic handling characteristics, there was a fair amount of turbo lag. Get into the throttle too early in a turn and the boost would rise and there would be more power than needed. Open the throttle too late and the boost pressure would not come up fast enough to have the desired speed coming out of the turn. A lot of finesse with the throttle was needed.

The overall appearance of the CX500TC was attention grabbing. With a white full fairing, colorful stripes, and gold-spoke cast wheels, this motorcycle would not be ignored. With the word Turbo on the front of the fairing and in large letters on each muffler, and *Honda* displayed prominently on each side of the fairing, the CX500TC made a very loud visual statement.

The CX500TC, like all of the turbo motorcycles, is very desirable and only slightly less sought after than the CX650T described next. Its sophistication and its history as the first of the factory turbos further enhance its desirability, and being a one-year model also makes the CX500TC quite rare. When buying a CX500TC, special attention needs to be given to the fairing, exhaust, and other items that were unique to this model. As with all turbocharged motorcycles, also be sure that the turbo is in good working order.

1983, CX650T (674 cc)

Collectibility	★★★★ 1/2
Passenger Accommodations	★★★
Reliability	★★★ 1/2
Parts/Service Availability	★★★
Handling	★★★
Engine Performance	★★★★ 1/2

Engine	twin cylinder, overhead valve, turbocharged four-stroke
Bore & stroke	82.5x63.0 mm
Displacement	674 cc
Compression ratio	7.8:1
Bhp at rpm	n/a
Transmission	5 speed
Primary drive	straight cut gear
Clutch	multi disc, wet plate
Brakes: front	twin disc, dual piston caliper
Brakes: rear	single disc, dual piston caliper
Tire size: front	100/90V18
Tire size: rear	120/90V17
Fuel capacity	5.3 gal
Wheelbase	58.9 in.
Weight	571 lb
Seat height	31.4 in.
Quarter-mile	11.75 sec at 112.21 mph*
Top Speed	139 mph*

*Cycle magazine test, October 1983

Not satisfied with the CX500TC, Honda introduced the CX650T only one year after the 500's debut. The basic engine layout of the 650 was the same as the 500, a longitudinally mounted turbocharged V-twin. In addition to the increase in displacement, the CX650T also had larger valves and a higher compression ratio than the 500. In order to tone down the effect of the boost coming on, the maximum boost pressure was lowered to 16.4 psi. To reduce the complexity of the CX500TC, the ignition sensor, atmospheric pressure sensor, and resonance chamber were eliminated on the

The 1983 CX650T was Honda's second turbocharged motorcycle. The engine monitoring and control systems were simplified, and other changes were made to take advantage of the benefits of the turbocharged engine. The styling remained very attention grabbing. *American Honda Motor Company*

CX650T. To simplify the electronics, the ignition control unit and the Computerized Fuel Injection were combined into one unit. The results of these changes were that the CX650T was quite a bit faster than the CX500TC and came closer to delivering the benefits expected of a turbocharged motorcycle. The CX650T did not, however, meet the public nor Honda's expectations and was not available the following year.

The styling of the CX650T was similar to the CX500TC, with a full fairing and slightly different stripping. There was still the "Turbo" identification on the front of the fairing and again in large letters on the exhaust. About the only significant difference in appearance between the two bikes was that the side covers denoted the CX650T as being a 650 rather than a 500.

The CX650T suspension was also similar to the CX500TC with the added benefit of three-way adjustable rebound dampening in the rear shock. Handling was similar to the CX500TC with the expected effects of the turbo lag.

The CX650T, being a turbo, is immediately a collectible motorcycle and one that seldom is seen for sale. Like the CX500TC, being a one-year model enhances its value and increases its scarcity. With its extra displacement and performance edge over the CX500TC, it ranks as one of the most collectible of the turbo motorcycles. Criteria for a desirable CX650T are much like those for the CX500TC. Look for a bike that has a fairing and other cosmetics that are in good condition and be sure that the turbocharger is functioning correctly.

Future collectibles
1985–1986, VF1000R (998 cc)

Collectibility	★★★
Passenger Accommodations	★★
Reliability	★★★★ 1/2
Parts/Service Availability	★★★★
Handling	★★★★
Engine Performance	★★★★ 1/2

Engine	V-4, dual overhead cam, four valve per cylinder, four-stroke
Bore & stroke	77x53.6 mm
Displacement	998 cc
Compression ratio	11:1
Bhp at rpm	117 at 10,000 (claimed)
Transmission	5 speed
Primary drive	straight cut gears
Clutch	multi disc, wet plate
Brakes: front	dual disc with dual piston calipers
Brakes: rear	single disc with single piston calipers
Tire size: front	120/80VR16
Tire size: rear	140/80V17
Fuel capacity	6.6 gal
Wheelbase	59.3 in.
Weight	587 lb
Seat height	31.9 in.
Quarter-mile	11.18 sec at 123.2 mph*
Top Speed	160 mph*

Motorcyclist magazine test, February 1985

The VF1000R was introduced in the U.S. market in 1985 as Honda's top-of-the-line Superbike. It had all the attributes needed to fill the position: a large, powerful, technically sophisticated engine; a full, racer style fairing; and a killer paint scheme. The VF1000R had been available in Europe in 1984, and prior to its introduction to the U.S. market it was anticipated to be a great improvement over the previous year's VF1000F.

The engine in the VF1000R was a four-valve, liquid-cooled V-four with dual overhead cams (DOHC). In a break with common Honda practice of using chain drive for the cams, the VF1000R cams were gear-driven. Being a 1000 cc V-four, the engine was very smooth and had a large amount of torque from the bottom to the top of the engine's rpm range.

The VF1000R suspension was fully adjustable and air assisted at both the front and the rear. Brakes were twin discs at the front with dual piston calipers and Honda's TRAC anti-dive system. The rear brake was a ventilated disc with a single piston caliper. Black Comstar wheels were used on both the front and the rear with—appropriate for the time—a high-tech, 16-inch front wheel.

The 1985 VF1000R was eagerly awaited by U.S. buyers for its great looks and anticipated high performance. While performance was very good, it was not as good as its competitors. The styling of the bike, though, was fantastic. This VF1000R is stock except for the Kerker exhaust. *Author's collection*

A view from the rear of the VF1000R, showing the interesting dual round taillights and the cover over the rear portion of the seat for solo riding. The tank pad is a period accessory. *Author's collection*

The 1985 VF1000R had a single square headlight. On the 1986 models this was changed to dual headlights. The headlight and a slight variation in the stripes are the only differences between the 1985 and 1986 models. *Author's collection*

The VF1000R was surrounded with a full fairing with a single square headlight (this changed to dual headlights in 1986) and fairing-mounted rearview mirrors. There was a removable tailpiece to cover the rear of the seat when riding solo. The red, white, and blue paint scheme of the VF1000R was fantastic, very eye catching, and made the looks of the bike very attractive.

The VF1000R was sold for only two years and in fairly small numbers. It was expensive, at $500 to $1,000 more than the other bikes in its class, and although its performance was excellent, it was not the best Superbike of the time. What the VF1000R does have going for it is good looks, a full fiberglass fairing, the technical intrigue of its gear-driven cams, and its relative scarcity. VF1000Rs can be found with some patience and persistence, and when found are very reasonably priced. As time passes and the VF1000R becomes harder to find, the value and asking prices for VF1000Rs will surely rise, and with them, its collectibility. If looking to buy a VF1000R, be sure to inspect the fairing carefully on any prospects. The VF1000R has a fiberglass fairing, which is easily damaged.

1989, GB500 Tourist Trophy (498 cc)

Collectibility	★★★ 1/2
Passenger Accommodations	★★
Reliability	★★★★ 1/2
Parts/Service Availability	★★★★
Handling	★★★ 1/2
Engine Performance	★★★

Engine	single cylinder, overhead cam, four-valve twin cylinder, four-stroke
Bore & stroke	92.0x75.0 mm
Displacement	498 cc
Compression ratio	8.9:1
Bhp	40 (claimed)
Transmission	5 speed
Primary drive	straight cut gears
Clutch	multi disc, wet plate
Brakes: front	twin-leading-shoe drum
Brakes: rear	single-leading-shoe drum
Tire size: front	90/90-18
Tire size: rear	110/90-18
Fuel capacity	4.5 gal
Wheelbase	55.6 in.
Weight	390 lb
Seat height	30.8 in.
Quarter-mile	14.19 sec at 92.4 mph*
Top Speed	109 mph*

*Motorcyclist magazine test, March 1989

It's rather hard to understand why Honda built a bike like the GB500. Its engine configuration, styling, and even its name tie to it an earlier time in motorcycle history, a time when bikes such as the BSA Gold Star were the sporting bikes of choice and the Isle of Man TT (Tourist Trophy) was the premier motorcycle event in the world. Sure, the GB500 is a retro-bike, but it also seems that there is more to it. It's like someone at Honda one day realized that Honda had never built a 500 cc single-cylinder sport bike, and decided that it needed to build one, and the GB500 was built to fill this perceived void.

The two main features of the GB500 were its engine and its styling. The engine in the GB500 was a 500 cc single-cylinder overhead-cam four-stroke. The head had four valves in what Honda called a Radial Four Valve Combustion chamber (RFVC). To dampen the vibration inherent in a big single, the engine was equipped with a gear-driven balancer shaft. For relief from the ritual usually required to start a big single, the GB500 was fitted with an electric start and an automatic compression release. Honda claimed an output of 40 horsepower for the engine.

The GB500 with its British-inspired styling and single-cylinder engine was a throwback to an earlier time, but still very much a Honda. The GB500 was only available in 1989 and 1990 and with its unusual styling and engine is sure to be a future collectible. *American Honda Motor Company*

The styling of the GB500 was very attractive, particularly if you were fond of British café racer styling. With wire spoke wheels, dual rear shocks, a separate speedometer and tachometer in chromed housings, the GB500 styling definitely originated in an earlier time. Add to this the small front fenders, clubman bars, the seat tailpiece, and the black green paint with gold pinstriping, and you had a bike that fitted the vision of what many people thought a motorcycle of the earlier era should look like. A very attractive motorcycle, indeed.

The GB500 was only available for two years and was made in relatively small numbers; however, with a little bit of searching, GB500s can be found for sale. A good indicator of the bike's desirability can be seen in its pricing. Currently, 10 years after the last GB500s were made and when the prices should be at their lowest, a well-maintained GB500 sells for as much as or more than it did when the bike was new. This lack of depreciation in value is a definite indicator that the GB500 has a devoted following and has strong potential to increase in value in the coming years. The GB500 is a reasonably new motorcycle, and any bike being considered for purchase should be in very good to excellent condition.

1990, VFR750R RC30 (748 cc)

1990 VFR750R RC30 (748 cc)	
Collectibility	★★★★ 1/2
Passenger Accommodations	N/A
Reliability	★★★★ 1/2
Parts/Service Availability	★★★
Handling	★★★★★
Engine Performance	★★★★★

	RC30
Engine	V-4, dual overhead cam, four valve per cylinder, four-stroke
Bore & stroke	70x48.6 mm
Displacement	748 cc
Compression ratio	11:1
Bhp at rpm	112 at 11,000
Transmission	6 speed
Primary drive	gear
Clutch	multi disc, wet plate
Brakes: front	twin disc
Brakes: rear	single disc
Tire size: front	120/70-17
Tire size: rear	170/60-18
Fuel capacity	4.7 gal
Wheelbase	55.5 in.
Weight	423 lb
Seat height	31 in.
Quarter-mile	n/a
Top Speed	155 mph (estimated)

The RC30 was an unusual bike for a Honda production street bike. While Honda is known for its mass-production assembly techniques and robotics, the RC30 was not built on Honda's normal assembly line. Instead, each RC30 was hand built by a small group of Honda Racing Corporation (HRC) employees. Hand assembly was very appropriate for the RC30, since it was a limited production racer-replica.

The engine in the RC30 was a 750 cc V-4 with four valves per cylinder, gear-driven overhead cams, liquid-cooling, and dual aluminum radiators. The racer influence was evident in the use of titanium for the connecting rods and a close-ratio six-speed transmission with a tall first gear. The rear end had a single-sided swingarm for lightness and quicker removal of the rear wheel. The RC30's frame was all aluminum, with the engine acting as a stressed member. The chassis dimensions, correct for a 750 race bike, were a 55.5 inch wheel base and 24 degrees of front rake. Included in the package was a pair of HRC cast-aluminum wheels. What it all added up to was that the RC30 was a hand-built race bike with the necessities to make it street legal—a concept very attractive to collectors.

The RC30 was available in the United States only in 1990 and in small numbers. Because of its limited production and its high level of performance, the RC30 is sure to be a future collectible. When new, the RC30 was expensive for a 750 cc sport bike and consequently tended to be well taken care of. As with all collectible bikes, though, you should be sure of the condition before buying. While RC30s don't show up in the local newspaper very often, they are offered for sale on a fairly regular basis in the specialty and collectors ads. When buying an RC30, look for a bike in near-perfect condition. These bikes are rare, were originally quite expensive, and should have had very good care and maintenance.

The VFR750R '90 RC30 was a street-legal racing bike made in small numbers and available only in 1990. Since it was immediately collectible, its future value is almost guaranteed. *American Honda Motor Company*

Chapter 2

Kawasaki

MODELS COVERED:

W1	S2 Mach II	KZ1300
A1 Samurai	Z1	KZ1000 R1 ELR
A7 Avenger	KZ900LTD	ZX750 Turbo
H1 Mach III	Z1R	ZX900 Ninja
H2 Mach IV	Z1RTC	ZX600 Ninja

The history of Kawasaki motorcycles is actually the history of two separate companies that came together in 1960 to build Kawasaki motorcycles. One of the companies is known today as Kawasaki Heavy Industries and the other was Meguro. These two companies both have complex histories that cannot be adequately covered in the space I have, so I will only hit the high points relating directly to Kawasaki motorcycles.

Meguro was founded in 1928 as a manufacturer of motorcycle transmissions. The intent of the establishment of the company was to become proficient in the manufacturing of motorcycle transmissions and to eventually manufacture complete motorcycles. By the mid-1930s, Meguro had reached the point that it was successful as a transmission manufacturer and was ready to undertake the manufacture of complete machines. In 1937, Meguro produced its first motorcycle: the 500 cc Z97, a copy of the Velocette MSS. During World War II, motorcycle production was interrupted, but following the war Meguro resumed manufacture of motorcycles and produced several new models, all of which proved to be very dependable and developed Meguro's reputation for reliability. Motorcycle production continued through the 1950s, and in 1960, Meguro brought out the motorcycle that would become a very important contributor to Kawasaki's lineup; the 500 cc K1. The K1, which eventually evolved into the Kawasaki W1, was, as Kawasaki says on its Web site, modeled heavily on the BSA A7.

Kawasaki's history starts in April 1878 when Shozo Kawasaki established a shipyard in Tsukiji, Tokyo. In the years between 1878 and World War II, Kawasaki expanded and diversified into many different product lines. In addition to ships, Kawasaki also built locomotives, produced steel, and—most important for its future in motorcycles—manufactured aircraft. After the interruption of World War II the various divisions of Kawasaki returned to their peacetime operations. The exception to this was the aircraft division, which had to find a new product to apply its engineering and manufacturing skills to.

The decision was made to produce and supply motorcycle transmissions to the many motorcycle manufacturers that sprang up in Japan after the war. This undertaking eventually led to the manufacture of complete engines and in 1953 to the establishment of Meihatsu to build and sell complete motorcycles. Meihatsu produced motorcycles for the next several years but with only limited success. In 1960 Kawasaki decided that action needed to be taken to improve its position as a motorcycle manufacturer, and a business relationship was established between the Kawasaki aircraft division and Meguro. In 1962, this partnership produced the first Kawasaki motorcycle, the B8. The following year Meguro and Kawasaki Aircraft Co. merged.

In order to expand its market in 1964, Kawasaki established an office in Los Angeles, California, and started importing motorcycles into the United States. Within two years of its start in the United States, Kawasaki introduced the 650 cc W1. In 1967, Kawasaki introduced the 250 cc A1 and the 350 cc A7, establishing its reputation as a manufacturer of high-performance motorcycles. In 1969 the 500 cc H1 was introduced, and it put Kawasaki on the map. These bikes, as well as many of the Kawasaki models that followed, have become classics.

The W1 was the largest displacement Japanese motorcycle made until the Honda CB750 came out. It was also Kawasaki's only four-stroke until the Z1 was introduced in 1973. *Copyright © 2000 Kawasaki Motor Corps. USA*

Rotary Valves

In the 1960s and early 1970s, the use of rotary disc valves on two-stroke street bikes was given a lot of attention. It was considered to be an important technical feature of high- performance two-stroke engines. When Kawasaki used rotary valves on the A1 and A7, the magazines made special note of this and explained the advantages attributed to rotary valves. When rotary valves were not used on the H1 and the other triples, the magazines again made note and took time and space to explain why and to comment on both the advantages and disadvantages of rotary valves.

In a piston-port two-stroke engine, the intake charge is drawn into the crankcase through the intake port on the back of the cylinder. The timing of the opening and closing of this port into the crankcase is controlled by the piston. Because of this, the relationship between the opening of the port and the closing of the port is fixed. Any modifications that are made to change the time when one of these events occurs will also change the other.

In a rotary valve engine, the intake charge is drawn in through a port in the side of the crankcase. The port is covered by a thin disc with a slot cut into it and attached to the end of the crankshaft. As the disc rotates, the slot passes over the port, opening it for the intake charge to pass into the crankcase. As the disc continues to rotate, the solid portion of the disc passes over the port, closing it. The timing of the opening and closing of the intake port are independent events determined by the position and length of the slot in the disc. This allows the timing and the duration of the intake to be changed by making changes to the disc

(continued on page 60)

(Continued from page 59)

slot. In addition, the rotary valve allows larger intake ports to be used than on a piston-port engine.

The main advantage to the use of a rotary valve is a broader power band when compared to a similar displacement piston-port engine. Additionally, though, a disc valve allows easier experimentation with intake timing. Get a few extra discs and open up the slot size or take a suitable disc from another engine—say, for example, put an A1 disc on an A7—and try them out. If you don't like the result you just put the stock disc back in. This is something that can't be done when you change the port size and shape with a Dremel tool on a piston-port engine.

The main disadvantage of the rotary valve is that the carburetor has to be situated on the end of the engine case, so that it feeds directly into the intake port. The carburetor thus adds to the overall engine width. This is obviously more pronounced on a twin-cylinder engine, and this extra width was something that the manufacturers worked hard to overcome. On a three-cylinder engine the use of disc valves was not practical since it would be extremely difficult to route the intake charge to the crankcase of the middle cylinder.

The right side of the W1, showing the separate transmission and the similarity of the engine and transmission to the BSA A10. *Copyright* © *2000 Kawasaki Motor Corps. USA*

1966–1971, W1, W1SS, W2SS, W2TT (624 cc)

Collectibility	★★★
Passenger Accommodations	★★★
Reliability	★★★
Parts/Service Availability	★★
Handling	★★ 1/2
Engine Performance	★★

Engine	twin cylinder, overhead valve, four-stroke
Bore & stroke	74x72.6 mm
Displacement	624 cc
Compression ratio	8.7:1
Bhp at rpm	50 at 6,500
Transmission	4 speed
Primary drive	duplex chain
Clutch	multi disc, wet plate
Brakes: front	twin-leading-shoe drum
Brakes: rear	single-leading-shoe drum
Tire size: front	3.25-18
Tire size: rear	3.50-18
Fuel capacity	4.0 gal
Wheelbase	55.7 in.
Weight	476 lb
Seat height	31.5 in.
Quarter-mile	15.6 sec at 85 mph*
Top Speed	101.2 mph*

Cycle World magazine test, August 1966

When the 650 cc W1 was introduced in 1966, it was not only the largest motorcycle in Kawasaki's lineup; it was also the largest motorcycle imported from Japan. The most noticeable thing about the W1 was its very close resemblance to the 650 cc BSA A10, which was produced from 1950 until 1963. This resemblance was due to the fact that the W1 was developed from the 500 cc Meguro K1, which was a copy of BSA's 500 cc A7. (The A7 was of the same basic engine design as the A10, just in a smaller displacement.) While there were detail differences between the W1 and the A10, their basic designs were very much alike.

While the W1 was a large displacement machine for the time, it was not performance oriented. The 650 cc parallel twin engine had a single carburetor and was in a mild state of tune. The W1's acceleration was not as quick as the British 650 twins or even 250 cc Suzuki X6 that was on the streets at this time. The suspension of the W1 was comparable to its engine performance. The ride was good and the handling was acceptable for recreational riding. The overall character of the machine was certainly more in line with the 1960s concept of touring rather than performance. While the W1 was a very capable machine, this lack of performance meant that the bike did not sell very well.

In 1968, improvements were made to the W1, resulting in two new models. The first was the W1SS, which had a redesigned head utilizing two carburetors. Styling was also updated with a tuck and roll seat, shorter front fender, and a restyled shorter exhaust. Interestingly, the new exhaust looked more like the exhaust on a BSA than the original W1 exhaust did.

The second new model for 1968 was the W2SS, which not only had the dual carb head, but also used larger valves and a slightly higher compression ratio to increase engine power from 50 to 53 horsepower. This power increase improved the acceleration of the bike and brought the quarter-mile time down into the mid 14-second range. Styling on the W2SS was also updated with the same exhaust and front fender as on the W1SS. The W2SS went a step further by having a painted gas tank and instruments that were separate from the headlight shell.

In 1969 Kawasaki brought out the final version of the W series, the W2TT, for the U.S. market. The W2TT was a typical street scrambler and had all the performance and styling improvements of the W2SS but also had a high level exhaust, with both pipes running down the left side of the bike.

The Kawasaki W series represents Kawasaki's efforts before it had found its place in the motorcycle market and developed a reputation for performance. All of the W bikes are desirable, with the W2s being slightly more so because of their increased performance. While they're not impossible to find, these bikes are not as common as some of Kawasaki's later models that sold in larger quantities. Be prepared to do some looking if you want to own either a W1 or a W2. When buying a W series Kawasaki, carefully consider the value of any missing or damaged parts. Locating parts for these bikes can require a long and time-consuming search.

The W2TT was the high-pipe version of the W2. This photo is from a W2TT brochure and differs in tank shape, exhaust, and seat detail from the W2TT photos in Kawasaki's Model Recognition Manual. *Copyright © 2000 Kawasaki Motor Corps. USA*

The 1967 A1 Samurai was the first of Kawasaki's two-stroke performance oriented motorcycles. Its rotary valve 250 cc twin-cylinder engine gave the A1 acceleration comparable to many larger displacement bikes. *Copyright © 2000 Kawasaki Motor Corps. USA*

1967–1971, A1/A1SS (247 cc)

In 1967 Kawasaki also brought out the A1SS street scrambler with the very stylish high pipes and braced handlebars. *Lou Demmel*

Collectibility	★★★ 1/2
Passenger Accommodations	★★
Reliability	★★★
Parts/Service Availability	★★ 1/2
Handling	★★ 1/2
Engine Performance	★★ 1/2

Engine	twin cylinder, rotary valve, two-stroke
Bore & stroke	53x56 mm
Displacement	247 cc
Compression ratio	7.0:1
Bhp at rpm	31 at 8,000
Transmission	5 speed
Primary drive	helical gear
Clutch	multi disc, wet plate
Brakes: front	twin-leading-shoe drum
Brakes: rear	single-leading-shoe drum
Tire size: front	3.00-18
Tire size: rear	3.25-18
Fuel capacity	3.5 gal
Wheelbase	51.0 in.
Weight	318 lb
Seat height	30.8 in.
Quarter-mile	15.4sec at 84.0 mph*
Top Speed	99 mph*

Cycle Guide magazine test, December 1966

In 1967, Kawasaki was still a relative newcomer to the motorcycle business. While the company was in production with models like the W1, Kawasaki was still looking for its place in the market and a bike to establish its image and reputation. The A1 was the bike that really started to carve a niche and was the first in a long procession of performance- oriented motorcycles from Kawasaki. While the W1 and its successors were considerably larger in displacement, they did not possess the performance or character of the A1.

A large part of the performance image, and what set the A1 apart from other bikes

The right side of the A1SS, showing the oil injection tank, the intake manifold feeding the carburetor under the engine side case, and the steering dampener. *Lou Demmel*

in the 250 class, came from the A1's engine configuration. While Bridgestone and Yamaha were both building rotary valve two-stroke singles at this time, the Kawasaki A1 was the first 250 cc rotary valve twin. With the rotary valves came associated advantages and disadvantages. The rotary valves allowed the intake timing to be optimized, giving the A1 a relatively broad power band for a two-stroke. However, because of the rotary valves, the carburetors were mounted on the sides of the engine and required relocation of the alternator and points, from the end of the crankshaft to behind the cylinders. This was done to maintain a reasonable engine width. Overall, Kawasaki overcame the problems posed by the rotary valves and made full use of the advantages they offered.

Performance for the A1 was quite good and enough to gain attention for Kawasaki. With its rotary valve engine and five-speed transmission, the A1 was capable of a quarter-mile time of under 15 1/2 seconds. With its brisk acceleration, the A1 was faster than the W1 and many other larger bikes, but with less than half the W1's displacement. Handling, while not as important to Kawasaki at this time as straight-line performance, was impressive for the era.

The A1 was also available starting in 1967 in street scrambler trim as the A1SS. The SS version of the A1 had braced handlebars, dual left side high-level exhaust, and an engine skid plate. Like most Street Scramblers of the time, the A1SS was predominantly an A1 in different trim, and there were no significant performance differences between the standard A1 and the A1SS. Street scramblers were in vogue at the time and the A1SS did look very cool and very much the part.

Although the A1's performance is not as spectacular as the A7's, the A1 is very significant as the first of Kawasaki's line of performance-oriented motorcycles. The A1 laid the foundation for Kawasaki's soon-to-be-established reputation as a designer and manufacturer of very quick, performance-above-all motorcycles. Today, A1s are not often seen and rarely come up for sale. Look for a complete A1 in good condition. This is another motorcycle that is difficult to find parts for.

A close-up of the Kawasaki winged flag tank emblem used through 1968. This emblem is on the A1SS. *Lou Demmel*

A close-up of the A1SS gauges showing the tachometer, speedometer, and warning lights all enclosed in a single instrument housing. *Lou Demmel*

Prior to the introduction of the Mach III the A7 Samurai was the fastest Kawasaki. Its rotary valve twin-cylinder two-stroke engine gave it outstanding performance for a 350 cc engine. This is a 1971 A7SS street scrambler. *Lou Demmel*

1967–1971, A7 Avenger (338 cc)

In 1969 Kawasaki significantly changed its styling, and the Kawasaki winged flag emblem was replaced by the Kawasaki name on the gas tank. This is a 1971 A7SS. *Lou Demmel*

Collectibility	★★★ 1/2
Passenger Accommodations	★★
Reliability	★★★
Parts/Service Availability	★★ 1/2
Handling	★★ 1/2
Engine Performance	★★ 1/2

Engine	twin cylinder, rotary valve, two-stroke
Bore & stroke	62x56 mm
Displacement	338 cc
Compression ratio	7.0:1
Bhp at rpm	40.5 at 7,500
Transmission	5 speed
Primary drive	helical gear
Clutch	multi disc, wet plate
Brakes: front	twin-leading-shoe drum
Brakes: rear	single-leading-shoe drum
Tire size: front	3.25-18
Tire size: rear	3.50-18
Fuel capacity	3.5 gal
Wheelbase	51.0 in.
Weight	325 lb
Seat height	31.8 in.
Quarter-mile	15.5 sec at 94 mph*
Top Speed	104 mph*

Cycle World magazine test, June 1967

A rear view of Lou's A7SS. The period license plate is a nice touch. *Lou Demmel*

Following closely behind the introduction of the A1 came the A7. The A7, with its 350 cc displacement, was very much like the A1, except that it was bigger, faster, and thus one step further in establishing Kawasaki's performance-oriented image.

The A7 engine was a twin-cylinder rotary-valve two stroke, similar to the A1. The main differences between the engines were an increase in the cylinder bore and larger carburetors, giving the A7 a power output of 42 horsepower. Changes were also made to the oil-injection system so that oil was not only injected into the intake tract, as on the A1, but also routed directly to the big end bearings. To go with the change in lubrication, the output of the oil pump was increased by 20 percent, and the lubrication system was given the Injectolube name.

Later in 1967, a street scrambler version of the A7 was introduced. The A7SS, as this model was designated, had the typical street scrambler items: braced handlebars, high exhaust running down the left side of the bike, and a skid plate. Otherwise the bike was the same as the street version of the A7, with the same acceleration and handling.

The A7 models with their added performance are slightly more desirable than the A1s; however, both A7s and A1s are rather difficult to find. If you desire one of these early twin-cylinder Kawasaki two-strokes, it would be best to purchase whichever model that you find first in reasonable condition.

1969–1976, H1 Mach III (498 cc)

Collectibility	★★★★
Passenger Accommodations	★★★
Reliability	★★ 1/2
Parts/Service Availability	★★★ 1/2
Handling	★★ 1/2
Engine Performance	★★★ 1/2

Engine	triple cylinder piston port, two-stroke
Bore & stroke	60x58.8 mm
Displacement	498 cc
Compression ratio	6.8:1
Bhp at rpm	60 at 8,000
Transmission	5 speed
Primary drive	gear
Clutch	multi disc, wet plate
Brakes: front	twin-leading-shoe drum
Brakes: rear	single-leading-shoe drum
Tire size: front	3.25-19
Tire size: rear	4.00-18
Fuel capacity	4.0 gal
Wheelbase	56.3 in.
Weight	415 lb
Seat height	31.4in.
Quarter-mile	13.2 sec at 100.22 mph*
Top Speed	119.14 mph*

Cycle World magazine test, April 1969

The 1969 H1 MACH III was one of the first Superbikes and firmly established Kawasaki as a builder of high-performance motorcycles. This 1969 H1 has been beautifully restored and even has the correct Dunlop Goldseal K77 tires. *Rick Seto*

The front view of an H1 shows the width of its engine and the narrowness of the tires of the late 1960s. *Rick Seto*

When the Mach III was introduced in 1969, it was one of the most radical motorcycles that had ever been made available to the public. Its uncompromising power and acceleration instantly solidified Kawasaki's reputation as a true performance-oriented motorcycle company. The other characteristics that accompanied the straight-line performance gave it a temperament that made it cherished by some, hated by just about as many, but never ignored by anyone involved in motorcycling at the time.

The heart of the H1 was its three-cylinder two-stroke engine. While the A1 and A7 were both equipped with rotary valves, the H1, due in part to its three-cylinder configuration, used pistonport induction. The H1's engine lubrication was by the Injectolube system, similar to the system used on the A7. Taking advantage of the three-cylinder engine configuration, the crank throws were set 120 degrees apart, giving the engine an inherent smoothness. Power for the triple

A closer view of the H1's engine shows the three individual spark plugs and the MACH III 500 side cover emblems. You can also see the ignition switch under the forward edge of the gas tank. *Rick Seto*

was rated at a very impressive 60 horsepower at 8,000 rpm. This was approximately 30 percent more than produced by the 500 cc Suzuki Titan engine. Equally as interesting as the total power output was the way the engine made its power—with an abrupt surge that occurred at about 6,000 rpm. This power surge was part of the distinctive character of the Kawasaki triples and was a major contributing factor to the H1's reputation. Also, as with all the Kawasaki triples, the H1's thirst for fuel was quite high, with fuel consumption figures of less than 30 miles per gallon being common.

The H1 was the first production motorcycle to use a Capacitor Discharge Ignition (CDI) system. The CDI system eliminated the points and associated problems found in a conventional ignition system. Also, the CDI system produced more-accurate ignition timing and higher voltage for the spark plugs. On the H1, surface gap spark plugs, together with the CDI, were used to eliminate the fouled spark plugs common with two-stroke engines of the time. While CDI systems offer many advantages and are widely used today, the H1's original CDI system was prone to problems, and when the CDI's "black box" failed, it seldom could be repaired and was expensive to replace. To overcome these problems, the H1's ignition system went through several changes, with the last change being for the 1974 model.

The chassis of the H1 was typical for the time and had nowhere near the sophistication of its engine. The frame was of rather light construction, which enhanced the power-to-weight ratio of the bike, but made the frame inadequate for the power produced by the engine. Handling woes like high-speed wobble, a tendency to want to come upright in a turn, and dragging the center stand in left-hand turns were some of the H1's more infamous handling traits. On the other hand, the brakes, although they did not have much feel, were quite effective. This was fortunate considering the way that most H1s were ridden. To further improve the situation, from 1972 on the H1 was equipped with a front disc brake.

The styling of the H1 was much sleeker looking than the earlier A7 or W1. The long gas tank was coupled with a long seat and turned-up tail. The bike was then complemented with an appealing paint scheme, which made for a very striking appearance. The most memorable view for many motorcycle riders of any of the Kawasaki triples, and particularly the H1, since it was the first, was from the rear. Where Suzuki would later use a symmetrical four-pipe exhaust on its triples, Kawasaki decided the straightforward approach was best and put one of the exhaust pipes on the left and two on the right. This asymmetrical setup gave the bike, when viewed from the rear, a very distinct and not easily forgotten appearance.

The H1 was a very significant motorcycle for Kawasaki, part of whose significance lay in its being one of the first superbikes. All of the H1s are desirable, but the earlier the better. The 1969s are the most desirable, with the other years spanning the spectrum down to the lower powered 1976 KH500, which is the least desirable. This is due partly to the fact that Kawasaki toned the bike down over the years and partly because the 1969 was the first of the lineage and built the reputation for the entire line. H1s are available on a fairly regular basis, but because of the H1's intended purpose, nearly all were originally owned by people who liked to drive them fast and hard. Extra care needs to be taken to be sure that the bike has been properly maintained and that the engine, clutch, and transmission are in good condition. Also be sure that the CDI system works properly and the exhaust system is correct and in good condition.

The rider's view of an H1. The enrichener lever for cold starting is inside and below the right hand grip. The friction steering dampener is adjusted by the black knob just below the instruments. *Rick Seto*

1972–1975, H2 Mach IV (748 cc)

Collectibility	★★★★
Passenger Accommodations	★★★
Reliability	★★★
Parts/Service Availability	★★★ 1/2
Handling	★★★
Engine Performance	★★★★

Engine	triple cylinder, piston port, two-stroke
Bore & stroke	71x63 mm
Displacement	748 cc
Compression ratio	7.0:1
Bhp at rpm	74 at 6,800
Transmission	5 speed
Primary drive	helical gear
Clutch	multi disc, wet plate
Brakes: front	single disc
Brakes: rear	single-leading-shoe drum
Tire size: front	3.25-19
Tire size: rear	4.00-18
Fuel capacity	4.5 gal
Wheelbase	55.4 in.
Weight	465 lb
Seat height	32.5 in.
Quarter-mile	12.72 sec at 103.8 mph*
Top Speed	119.72 mph*

Cycle World magazine test, March 1972

The H1 Mystique

What made the H1 so well known, so notorious, and so desirable today were all of the different aspects of the bike taken as a whole. While its sheer acceleration and the fact that it was one of the fastest things on the street in 1969 would make the H1 a memorable motorcycle, it was the way that it went fast that added to its attraction and mystique. When the power surge at 6,000 rpm would hit, the front end would come up and severely scare an uninitiated rider. Hit this power surge in the middle of a corner and it could become more than just scary—you could quickly find yourself in the bushes.

When the bike was ridden by an experienced rider, its performance was spectacular. Bring the revs up, move forward on the bike so that the wheelie could be controlled and let out the clutch. The front end would come up and the bike would take off. Shift through the gears when the tach hit redline and you went for a very quick ride. While the rider was staying busy shifting through the gears and controlling this event, there was not a single person anywhere along the street that could possibly miss what was going on. The sound of the engine being revved for the launch would grab people's attention. When people turned to look for the source of the noise, they would be greeted by the sight of the H1 with its front wheel in the air accelerating fiercely away. This vision, together with the shrieking sound of the three-cylinder engine and the trail of smoke, was spectacular. It was an experience that was quickly over for both the rider and the spectator, but it was something that was never forgotten by anyone who ever rode an H1 or witnessed it being put to its intended use.

With the introduction of the MACH IV and the MACH II to join the very successful MACH III, Kawasaki proclaimed 1972 the "year of the tri-stars" and passed out this brochure with the three triples on the cover. *Copyright © 2000 Kawasaki Motor Corps. USA*

Following on the success of the MACH III was the 1972 750 cc MACH IV, now more commonly known as the H2. With its larger engine, the H2 was even faster than the H1 and bumped the requirements to be a Superbike up another notch. *Copyright © 2000 Kawasaki Motor Corps. USA*

While the H1 established Kawasaki's reputation as a leading manufacturer of high-performance motorcycles, the H2 solidly reinforced that reputation. The H2 was very much like the H1 except that it had larger displacement, made more power, and made it more quickly. What the H1 did, the H2 did in a bigger way.

The engine in the H2 was the same basic design as the other Kawasaki two-stroke triples. The H2 engine was scaled up. The bore was larger and the stroke was increased to get the added displacement. The compression ratio was also slightly higher in the H2 and the carburetors were of a larger diameter. The result of these differences was that the H2, rated at 74 horsepower, had about 25 percent more horsepower than the H1. The H2 was more civilized and made its power over a broader rpm range than the H1. Straight-line performance was also better—the H2 was almost a half-second quicker in the quarter-mile than the H1. One thing that was not improved was fuel consumption: The H2 was even thirstier, getting around six miles less per gallon than the H1.

The chassis of the H2 was enhanced with larger frame tubes, more substantial bracing, and improved front forks. While it was an improvement over the H1, the H2—particularly the early ones—still exhibited rather undesirable handling characteristics as the speed went up. Fortunately, the H2 was introduced the same year that Kawasaki started using disc brakes on the triples and was fitted with a single-disc front brake.

Styling for the first year H2 was attractive and more like that of the smaller 250 cc S1 and 350 cc S2 than the H1. Like the smaller triples, the H2 had the exhaust angled up and a tailpiece behind the seat. All triples, though, shared the distinctive asymmetrical exhaust system first seen on the H1.

The H2 is a desirable motorcycle that built on the notoriety of the H1 and further enhanced Kawasaki's reputation for performance. Also, the H2, being bigger and faster, could arguably put on a better show than an H1, and its reputation and desirability are at least partially based on this fact. Availability of H2s is not quite as good as H1s, but H2s can be found for sale on a fairly regular basis. Desirability of different year H2s is similar to that of H1s: The early H2s made more power and are more desirable than the later H2s. The H2 buyer needs to remember that most H2s have very likely been owned at some time or another by someone who rode the bike fast and hard. Extra care needs to be taken to be sure that any bike being considered for purchase has been properly cared for and is in good order mechanically. Also, be sure the three-pipe exhaust system is in good condition, as these can be difficult to replace.

This is the front of a 1972 "year of the tri-stars" sales brochure for the H2 MACH IV. *Copyright © 2000 Kawasaki Motor Corps. USA*

1972–1973, S2 Mach II (346 cc)

Collectibility	★★★
Passenger Accommodations	★★ 1/2
Reliability	★★★
Parts/Service Availability	★★★
Handling	★★★
Engine Performance	★★ 1/2

Engine	triple cylinder, piston port, two-stroke
Bore & stroke	53x52.3 mm
Displacement	346 cc
Compression ratio	7.3:1
Bhp at rpm	45 at 8,000
Transmission	5 speed
Primary drive	gear
Clutch	multi disc, wet plate
Brakes: front	twin-leading-shoe drum
Brakes: rear	single-leading-shoe drum
Tire size: front	3.00-18
Tire size: rear	3.50-18
Fuel capacity	3.7 gal
Wheelbase	52.5 in.
Weight	346 lb
Seat height	30.5 in.
Quarter-mile	15.10 sec at 83.79 mph*
Top Speed	91.64 mph*

*Cycle World magazine test, September 1971

The 1972 S2, the 350 cc version of the Kawasaki triple. This ad proclaims another Kawasaki first, "the TriStar Triple 350" with "rocket-thrust acceleration." Copyright © 2000 Kawasaki Motor Corps. USA

The 1972 S2 with its piston-port three-cylinder engine and five-speed transmission. Lou Demmel

A right rear view of the S2 shows the asymmetrical three-pipe exhaust used on the Kawasaki triples. Lou Demmel

The S2 was the smaller, tamer version of the Kawasaki triple. While still quick for its size, and very sporting in both appearance and performance, it was not as brutish as the larger triples.

Just as the 750 cc H2 was a scaled-up version of the 500 triple, the 350 cc S2 was a scaled-down version. The bore was smaller and the stroke was shorter to obtain the 350 cc displacement. The carburetors were also smaller. Differing from the larger triples, the S2 did not use a CDI system but rather handled the ignition by three sets of breaker points. The result of these changes was that the S2 was rated at 45 horsepower, or 15 horsepower less than the H1. While the engine made less power than the H1, it still had the same power surge in the 6,000 rpm range and the same sporting nature.

Handling on the S2 was not perfect, but it wasn't as wild as the H1. This was probably due as much to the lighter weight and less power to deal with than any drastic improvements in the chassis components. Brakes on the 1972 S2 were drum, front and rear, unlike the larger triples, but they were upgraded to a front disc the following year.

Other versions of the S series were also made, with the 250 cc S1 Mach I also being introduced in 1972. This version was a further scaled-down version of the triple with lower power and even more civilized behavior. The bore on the 1974 S2 was increased to produce the 400 cc S3.

Because of their smaller size and tamer character, the S2 and the other S models are not as sought after as the bigger triples. Due to this lower demand, the S models are not seen for sale as often as the H1s and H2s. Nonetheless, the S2 is a desirable motorcycle, exhibiting the most appealing characteristics of the larger triples in a smaller, more civilized package. Look for an S2 in good condition with a good original exhaust system, since parts for S2s can be more difficult to find than parts for an H1 or H2.

1973–1975, Z1 (903 cc)

In 1973 Kawasaki introduced the new king of the Superbikes, the Z1. Its dual overhead cam 903 cc four-stroke engine made it the fastest motorcycle on the street and signaled the impending end of Kawasaki's two-stroke street bikes. *Bob Shue*

Collectibility	★★★★ 1/2
Passenger Accommodations	★★★★
Reliability	★★★★
Parts/Service Availability	★★★ 1/2
Handling	★★★ 1/2
Engine Performance	★★★★

Engine	four cylinder, dual overhead cam, four-stroke
Bore & stroke	66x66 mm
Displacement	903 cc
Compression ratio	8.5:1
Bhp at rpm	82 at 8,500
Transmission	5 speed
Primary drive	gear
Clutch	multi disc, wet plate
Brakes: front	single disc
Brakes: rear	single-leading-shoe drum
Tire size: front	3.25-19
Tire size: rear	4.00-18
Fuel capacity	4.7gal
Wheelbase	59.0 in.
Weight	543 lb
Seat height	32 in.
Quarter-mile	12.61sec at 105.63 mph*
Top Speed	120 mph*

Cycle World magazine test, March 1973

Although the Z1 was introduced to the U.S. motorcycle market in 1973, it was a project that Kawasaki had been working on since 1967. The intent of the project, code-named New York Steak (or NYS, as the magazines dubbed it), was to build a very polished and sophisticated large, fast motorcycle. The motorcycle would not have the roughness of the two-stroke triples or any inherent flaws that the rider had to tolerate to own and ride what would be the fastest motorcycle on the street. Originally conceived as a four-cylinder 750, the project was delayed and revised when Honda, to Kawasaki's surprise, introduced the CB750 in 1969. After seeing the positive response that the Honda received, Kawasaki decided that its initial idea had been right, but some of the details of the project needed to be changed. Kawasaki did not want the NYS to be perceived as a copy of the Honda but rather a clearly distinctive, indisputably superior motorcycle. It was decided that the displacement of the NYS would be increased to 900 cc to insure that it would produce more power than the 750 Honda. Many different styling concepts were also looked at to ensure the new bike would have a look different than the Honda's. When all of the design, styling, and testing were completed, the Z1 was put into production. Kawasaki had a bike for sale that was everything that it had dreamed of.

What gave the Z1 its power and much of its character was its 903 cc four-cylinder dual overhead cam (DOHC) engine. With the exception of perhaps the dual cams, the engine, like most of the rest of the Z1, was not so much new and radical but rather a result of well-thought-out applications of ideas already in use. The dual overhead cam, while not a totally new idea, was not common at the time in mass-produced motorcycles. The DOHC configuration eliminated the rocker arms and allowed the cams to operate directly on followers on the ends of the valve stems, providing more accurate valve control at higher engine speeds. Adjusting the valve clearances with this arrangement required measuring and replacing shims. This was more complicated than the rocker arm screw adjusters commonly used at that time. Over time, this arrangement proved to be very reliable and not really that hard to adjust. After the introduction of the Z1, the dual overhead cam engine became widely used by all motorcycle manufacturers.

Other features of the engine included four separate carburetors to feed the four cylinders and the use of regular low-octane gasoline. Due to rising concerns at the time over engine emissions, the engine was also designed to meet all existing, as well as all anticipated, emissions requirements. The engine produced 82 horsepower, which was fed to the rear wheel through a five-speed transmission and chain final drive. Performance was spectacular. Quarter-mile times in the low 12-second region were common, with a top speed of around 130 miles per hour. The Z1's acceleration and top speed were what made it the king of the Superbikes.

Early test reports on the Z1 talked about excellent handling and how cornering was only limited in left-hand turns by the center stand hitting the pavement. Overall, handling on the Z1 was very good, particularly for a big street bike—but not perfect. For most riding, the bike behaved reasonably well, but the Z1 was very fast and when ridden near its limit, could be a handful. Because of its size, if any-thing went wrong, it was difficult to bring the bike back under control. Overall, the Z1's engine technology was quite a bit ahead of its chassis technology.

The brakes on the Z1 were very capable. A single disc was mounted on the left front fork tube, and there were mounting lugs on the right fork tube so that a second disc could be added. This second set of mounting lugs was apparently in anticipation of the inevitable adoption of dual disc front brakes. Braking at the rear was handled by a drum brake setup.

A close-up of the Z1's side cover announcing its Double Overhead Camshaft 900 engine. *Bob Shue*

Not only did the Z1 engine make for a very fast motorcycle, but the engine was also impressive looking with its large size, dual overhead camshafts, and four exhaust pipes. *Bob Shue*

Styling of the Z1 needed to be different from the CB750 and appropriate to the stature of the motorcycle that Kawasaki intended it to be. Its look was sleek, from the line of the unbraced front fender and tapered gas tank to the slim side covers and tail section. The exhaust was four separate pipes and mufflers angled upwards with the ends cut perpendicular to the ground, giving it a distinctive look. The look of the engine made it obvious that this was a large displacement motorcycle. Altogether, the result was distinctive and left the viewer with no doubt that this was a fast, prestigious motorcycle.

In 1977, the Z1 engine was enlarged to 1,000 cc for the KZ1000 and there were several variations of both the 900 cc and the 1,000 cc models. A few of the more significant of these bikes are covered later in this book.

All of the 900 cc Kawasakis are collectible and can be found with a moderate amount of searching. It's best to follow the "earlier the better" rule, with the 1973 Z1s being most desirable. As is the case with the purchase of most collectible Japanese motorcycles, when buying a Z1 it is important to be sure that the gas tank, fenders, and all of the body work are correct for the bike. Also, on a Z1 the original exhaust system is an important part of the value of the bike, since original Z1 exhaust systems are difficult to find and are expensive to purchase.

1975–1976, KZ900LTD (903 cc)

Collectibility	★★★
Passenger Accommodations	★★★ 1/2
Reliability	★★★★
Parts/Service Availability	★★★
Handling	★★★ 1/2
Engine Performance	★★★★

Engine	four cylinder, dual overhead cam, four-stroke
Bore & stroke	66x66 mm
Displacement	903 cc
Compression ratio	8.5:1
Bhp at rpm	81 at 8,500
Transmission	5 speed
Primary drive	gear
Clutch	multi disc, wet plate
Brakes: front	dual disc
Brakes: rear	single disc
Tire size: front	3.50H19
Tire size: rear	5.10H16
Fuel capacity	3.4 gal
Wheelbase	59.5 in.
Weight	514 lb (dry)
Seat height	n/a
Quarter-mile	n/a
Top Speed	120 est.

Up through the mid-1970s, Japanese motorcycles were not made with the specialized model variations that we have today. Even bikes that were performance oriented and labeled as Superbikes were not much different in appearance from non-Superbikes. The same was true with cruisers. Motorcycles were sold unadorned, and it was up to the owner to modify or accessorize the bike as was appropriate for its intended use. Aftermarket fairings, seats, handlebars, exhaust, and numerous other items were available, but it was up to the individual owner to buy these items and install them or have them installed. This meant that after buying a new bike there was still more money to be spent to buy the desired parts and time to be spent installing the parts. To make matters worse, this situation meant that many good parts were removed from the bike in order to install the new aftermarket items. Today, these removed parts are often what separates a valuable vintage Japanese motorcycle from a parts bike.

With the KZ900LTD, Kawasaki changed this situation. The KZ900LTD (LTD standing for Limited) was the first of the factory-made custom motorcycles and started the class of motorcycles now referred to as cruisers. The LTD made it possible for a buyer to go into a Kawasaki dealer and buy a motorcycle with many of the more popular aftermarket items already installed. After the success of the KZ900LTD, other manufacturers, such as Yamaha with its Specials, and Suzuki with its "L series," followed suit and brought out their own line of custom bikes.

The LTD used the stock KZ900 engine, transmission, and chain drive but the exhaust was changed to a Jardine four-into-two that fed into megaphone-shaped mufflers. For the right look and riding position, a stepped seat and pull-back handlebars were used. Dual disc brakes were installed in the front and a single disc at the rear. Mullholland shocks replaced the stock rear shock absorbers while the front forks remained as on the stock KZ900. To complete the package, a shortened front fender was used, the gas tank was smaller and slimmed down, and a 16-inch rear wheel was fitted. All of these custom parts added up to a very appealing motorcycle for the many potential buyers that were interested in this style of motorcycle.

As the first factory-made custom motorcycle, the KZ900LTD introduced a new style of motorcycle models. The LTD, together with the sport-oriented models like the Z1R, played a role in the current practice of building very specialized motorcycles to meet the demands of the various niches in the motorcycle marketplace.

In 1977 the engine on the LTD was enlarged to 1,000 cc. Being made in limited quantities for only one year, the KZ900LTD is a rare bike. If you are looking for an example of one of the first cruisers, the KZ900LTD should be given serious consideration. Be sure that the exhaust is the original Jardine system and the shocks are Mullhollands, as these items are both very hard to find and nearly impossible to duplicate.

The 1976 KZ900LTD with its step seat, megaphone pipes, and special paint may look rather sedate today but in 1976 it was quite radical. The KZ900LTD was the predecessor to today's cruisers. Copyright © 2000 Kawasaki Motor Corps. USA

The KZ1000LTD continued on in the style of the KZ900LTD. The Kawasaki LTDs led to the present cruiser section of the motorcycle market. This is a 1980 KZ1000LTD. Copyright © 2000 Kawasaki Motor Corps. USA

1978–1980, Z1R (1,016 cc)

The Z1R with its small fairing and angular styling was, like the KZ900LTD, another indicator of things to come. *Copyright © 2000 Kawasaki Motor Corps. USA*

Collectibility	★★★★ 1/2
Passenger Accommodations	★★★ 1/2
Reliability	★★★★
Parts/Service Availability	★★★
Handling	★★★ 1/2
Engine Performance	★★★★

Engine	four cylinder, dual overhead cam, four-stroke
Bore & stroke	70x66 mm
Displacement	1016 cc
Compression ratio	8.7:1
Bhp at rpm	90 at 8,000
Transmission	5 speed
Primary drive	gear
Clutch	multi disc, wet plate
Brakes: front	dual disc
Brakes: rear	single disc
Tire size: front	3.50H18
Tire size: rear	4.00H18
Fuel capacity	3.9 gal
Wheelbase	59.4 in.
Weight	549 lb
Seat height	31.9 in.
Quarter-mile	12.13 sec at 109.6 mph*
Top Speed	132 mph*

*Cycle Guide magazine test, January 1978

When the Z1R was introduced, it was another bike, like the KZ900LTD, that indicated where the future of motorcycles was headed. In 1978, with most bikes being styled very much alike, there was still not a major distinction between sport bikes, standard bikes, and cruisers. While the essence of the Z1R was mainly styling, it was a definite step toward developing and marketing different styles of motorcycles for distinctly different purposes.

The Z1R engine was the same as the contemporary KZ1000 except for the carburetors and exhaust. The carburetors were slightly larger by 2 millimeters and the exhaust was a four-into-one rather than the KZ1000's standard four-into-two. Kawasaki claimed about an 8-percent horsepower increase for these changes.

The chassis components were slightly changed from the KZ1000, with some improvements to the frame and firmer rear shocks. Braking was by dual front and single rear drilled disc. The seven-spoke cast wheels on the Z1R were made by Kawasaki. The effect of these changes was fairly minor, and the result was that the straight-line performance and handling of the Z1R was comparable to the KZ1000.

The addition of a fairing allowed for more gauges. In addition to the speedometer, tachometer, and warning lights, the fairing housed an ampmeter and a fuel gauge. The front brake master cylinder was mounted down behind the fairing rather than up on the handlebars. A cable that ran from the brake lever down to the master cylinder actuated the brakes.

The area where the Z1R was significantly different was in styling. The most obvious item was the small handlebar-mounted fairing that gave the Z1R its café racer look. The fairing's angular styling was carried through the other major components that gave the bike its appearance. The gas tank, tail section, and side covers all had a sharp-edged crispness and lines that flowed smoothly together. The drilled discs, cast wheels, and four-into-one exhaust ail complemented the café racer appearance.

The Z1R was not the fastest thing on the street in 1978. The Yamaha XS11 held that title, but the Z1R was definitely one of the sportiest looking. While Z1Rs are fairly rare bikes, if you are a fan of the big Kawasaki four-cylinder bikes and want something that looks different from the other bikes from this time period, the Z1R is definitely a must-have. When buying a Z1R, be sure that items unique to this model, such as fairing and side covers, are present and in good condition.

1978–1979, Z1RTC Turbo (1,016 cc)

Collectibility	★★★★ 1/2
Passenger Accommodations	★★★
Reliability	★★ 1/2
Parts/Service Availability	★★ 1/2
Handling	★★★
Engine Performance	★★★★★

Engine	four cylinder, dual overhead cam, four-stroke
Bore & stroke	70x66 mm
Displacement	1016 cc
Compression ratio	n/a
Bhp at rpm	n/a
Transmission	5 speed
Primary drive	gear
Clutch	multi disc, wet plate
Brakes: front	dual disc
Brakes: rear	single disc
Tire size: front	3.50-18
Tire size: rear	4.00-18
Fuel capacity	3.4 gal
Wheelbase	59.4 in.
Weight	558 lb
Seat height	31.9 in.
Quarter-mile	10.90 sec at 130 mph*
Top Speed	n/a

*Motorcyclist magazine test, August 1978

The Z1RTC was the predecessor to the factory turbo bikes. It was fast, very impressive looking, and now very collectible but it was only half Kawasaki. This is the 1979 version with the wild paint scheme.
Martin Landry

The Z1RTC is somewhat out of place here, since it was not completely manufactured by Kawasaki. The Z1RTC was based on the Z1R though and was produced in sufficient quantities to be considered more than a special-order custom. The Z1RTC was also a significant model, foretelling the future path for performance motorcycles and serving as a direct predecessor to the factory turbos that were to come out only a few years later. Also, the Z1RTC is unquestionably collectible.

The Z1RTC was a standard Kawasaki Z1R to which an American Turbo-Pak turbocharger was added. The turbochargers were installed by Turbo Cycle Corporation and the completed motorcycles were sold through a small group of Kawasaki dealers.

Since neither the Z1R engine nor chassis were designed for the turbocharger, however, there were problems. With the power available and the turbo lag, the handling could be very tricky. Also, if the waste gate was adjusted to get even more power out of the engine, which was quite doable, the engine life could be very short. This was made all the more interesting by the fact that the Z1RTCs were sold without any form of warranty. The turbocharger did accomplish exactly what it was intended to do; it made the bike very fast in a straight line. Quarter-mile times of around 11 seconds were common.

Even with the problems, though, the Z1RTC became a very collectible motorcycle. The short, two-year life and low production numbers (approximately 1,000 were built) together with the Z1RTC's reputation for outrageous acceleration make this bike a very desirable collectible today. If the Z1RTC is a bike that you must have for your collection, be prepared to spend some time searching, however, as these bikes are quite rare. And as with all turbo motorcycles, be sure that the turbocharger and all associated plumbing is in good working order when considering a Z1RTC for purchase.

1979–1989, KZ1300 (1,286 cc)

Collectibility	★★★
Passenger Accommodations	★★★★
Reliability	★★★★
Parts/Service Availability	★★★
Handling	★★★ 1/2
Engine Performance	★★★★

Engine	six cylinder liquid cooled, four-stroke
Bore & stroke	62x71 mm
Displacement	1286 cc
Compression ratio	9.9:1
Bhp at rpm	120 at 8,000
Transmission	5 speed, shaft final drive
Primary drive	HyVo chain
Clutch	multi disc, wet plate
Brakes: front	dual disc
Brakes: rear	single disc
Tire size: front	110/90-18
Tire size: rear	130/90-17
Fuel capacity	5.63 gal
Wheelbase	62.48 in.
Weight	710 lb
Seat height	31.85 in.
Quarter-mile	11.96 sec at 114.35 mph*
Top Speed	135 mph*

*Cycle magazine test, March 1979

The engine of the KZ1300 was an interesting sight with its finless cylinders, six exhaust pipes, and large radiator.

The KZ1300 with its six-cylinder engine was a large, fast motorcycle best suited to covering long distances. The appeal of the angular styling was very much a matter of taste.

Bob Shue's one-owner, beautifully maintained original 1983 KZ1000R Eddie Lawson Replica. The Eddie Lawson Replica had all of the necessary ingredients to make it an instant classic; great looks, superb acceleration, excellent handling, and limited production, plus association with a famous name. This 1983 ELR has the Kerker decal, which was included with the bike, affixed to the gas tank, as was common with many ELRs. *Bob Shue*

The gas tank of the ELR proudly displays the decal proclaiming Kawasaki's 1981–1982 Superbike Championship and the fact that this is a Superbike Replica. *Bob Shue*

The KZ1300 was Kawasaki's large six-cylinder motorcycle for the late 1970s. Although having a six-cylinder engine like the Honda CBX, the KZ1300 was different in many aspects and was an entirely different type of motorcycle from the CBX. While the CBX was a sport bike that in its last two years of production became a sports tourer, the KZ1300 from its introduction was a large sports tourer or touring bike.

The KZ1300's engine was a six-cylinder with dual overhead cams, liquid cooling, and a power output rating of 120 horsepower. The drivetrain was a five-speed transmission and shaft final drive. The KZ1300, as would be expected, was fast, with a top speed of more than 130 miles per hour. But speed and acceleration were only part of the appeal. This was a bike that could not only travel very quickly over long distance but could also carry two people comfortably with as much gear as they wanted to bring. In addition to the bike's speed and load-carrying capability, the gas tank capacity was over five and a half gallons, giving the KZ1300 excellent cruising range.

Styling of the KZ1300 was rather boxy with its rectangular headlight and sharply creased gas tank, side covers, and tail section. Add to this its angular fenders, finless cylinders and head, rectangular radiator, and rectangular turn signals, and you had a very imposing motorcycle.

The KZ1300 is a large, fast, very capable long-distance motorcycle. The six-cylinder 1300 cc engine is technically interesting, very strong, and does an excellent job of pulling this motorcycle along in style. If you're looking for a large, impressive six-cylinder motorcycle and you think the CBX is too common and doesn't do it for you, then the KZ1300 may be just the thing. When looking at a KZ1300 for possible purchase, pay close attention to the condition of the exhaust system, since replacement original exhaust components will be very difficult to find and very costly to buy if you are fortunate enough to locate them.

1982–1983, KZ1000R1, Eddie Lawson Replica (998 cc)

The instruments of the ELR, showing the tachometer, speedometer, fuel gauge, and warning lights as well as the covered Schraeder valves for the air adjustable suspension. The 2,497 miles on the odometer are accurate on this bike. The BREAK-IN CAUTION sticker still attached to the tachometer face is a nice touch for an original bike. *Bob Shue*

Collectibility	★★★★ 1/2
Passenger Accommodations	★★★
Reliability	★★★★
Parts/Service Availability	★★★
Handling	★★★★ 1/2
Engine Performance	★★★★

Engine	four cylinder, dual overhead cam, four-stroke
Bore & stroke	69.4x66.0 mm
Displacement	998 cc
Compression ratio	9.2:1
Bhp at rpm	79.01 at 8,500*
Transmission	5 speed
Primary drive	spur gear
Clutch	multi disc, wet plate
Brakes: front	dual disc
Brakes: rear	single disc
Tire size: front	100/90X19
Tire size: rear	120/90X18
Fuel capacity	5.7 gal
Wheelbase	60.0 in.
Weight	543.5 lb
Seat height	30.5 in.
Quarter-mile	11.72 sec at 114.06 mph*
Top Speed	138 mph*

Cycle magazine test, November 1982

The KZ1000R1, better known as the Eddie Lawson Replica or ELR, was produced by Kawasaki to commemorate Eddie Lawson's 1981 Superbike championship. With the ELR, Kawasaki produced not only a very eye-catching motorcycle, but also one of the better sport bikes of the early 1980s.

The ELR was based on the standard KZ1000J, Kawasaki's very fast standard street model in 1982. There were similarities between the two machines but there were also many differences that make the ELR a very distinct motorcycle. The most noticeable difference was that the ELR had a small fairing and a bright Kawasaki lime-green paint scheme

The 1984 ZX750E1 Turbo was not only fast but looked the part, with its full fairing and spoiler midsection separating the upper and lower fairing halves. *Bob Shue*

with blue and white stripes. Also, the gas tank was more square and not teardrop shaped like the KZ1000J. The ELR seat had a more pronounced step in it and had a nose that went up and covered the back of the gas tank.

Beyond its striking appearance, there were many functional details that were changed and upgraded to give the ELR its sporting character. The engine was the same as the standard KZ1000J engine with the addition of the oil cooler that was used on the GPZ1100. The exhaust was a four-into-one Kerker setup with the Kerker name displayed very prominently on the side of the muffler. The choice of the Kerker exhaust was directly related to Kerker's sponsorship of Kawasaki's championship-winning Superbike team. Because of the Kerker exhaust, the ELR had no center stand.

Modifications were also made to the chassis to improve the handling. The rake angle of the forks was increased and the fork dampening was changed, making the forks stiffer. In the back, special gas-charged shocks with separate reservoirs were used, which stiffened up the rear suspension. Along with these suspension changes came rear-set footpegs and specially shaped handlebars, making for a very comfortable riding position. The suspension setup worked great when the bike was used as intended and ridden fast. When ridden at low speeds, though, the suspension was harsh and said to be similar to the 1982 Suzuki Katana for lack of ride comfort.

The ELR was produced in 1982 and 1983 in limited quantities. The limited production, together with the ELR's looks and sporting character, have made the ELR a very collectible but rare motorcycle. Since the ELR was essentially collectible from the time it was introduced, many of the bikes were well taken care of and have survived in excellent condition. If you encounter an ELR that is in less than perfect condition, be sure that all of the ELR unique parts are there. The price of a less than complete bike may make it tempting, but the parts search could prove to be very difficult.

A rear view of the 750 Turbo with the tail "uni-trak" decal announcing the rear suspension system. The rectangular display on the top of the gas tank is an LCD fuel gauge and warning indicators. The smaller rectangular display above the instruments is the Boost gauge. *Bob Shue*

1984–1985, ZX750 E1 Turbo (738 cc)

The ZX750E1Turbo right side cover.
Bob Shue

Collectibility	★★★★
Passenger Accommodations	★★★
Reliability	★★★
Parts/Service Availability	★★★
Handling	★★★
Engine Performance	★★★★★

Engine	four cylinder, DOHC, turbocharged, four-stroke
Bore & stroke	66.0x54.0 mm
Displacement	738 cc
Compression ratio	7.8:1
Bhp at rpm	112 at 9,000
Transmission	5 speed
Primary drive	HyVo chain and straight cut gear
Clutch	multi disc, wet plate
Brakes: front	dual disc
Brakes: rear	single disc
Tire size: front	110/90V19
Tire size: rear	130/80V18
Fuel capacity	4.5 gal
Wheelbase	58.7 in.
Weight	556 lb
Seat height	30.7 in.
Quarter-mile	11.13 sec at 120.32 mph*
Top Speed	161 mph*

*Cycle magazine test, November 1983

Kawasaki, like the other three major Japanese manufacturers, decided in the mid-1980s that it was necessary to build a turbocharged motorcycle. Like the turbo bikes from the other manufacturers, the Kawasaki turbo was very short-lived, made only in 1984 and 1985. Kawasaki, like the other Japanese manufacturers, quickly learned that the future of motorcycling was not in turbocharging.

The 750 Turbo was based on Kawasaki's sporting 750 of the time, the GPz 750. The turbocharger was mounted to the front of the engine below the exhaust ports. The four exhaust pipes came together at the top of the turbocharger and fed the engine exhaust into the turbocharger. The exhaust then left the turbocharger by a single pipe on the right side that split into two pipes to feed the two mufflers. The air intake for the engine was through a housing on the left side of the engine toward the rear. The air came in through an opening in the housing, through an air filter, then went forward into a pipe that fed into the turbocharger. From the turbocharger, the air went back through a pipe on the left side of the cylinders, fed into the

The 1984 900 Ninja was an excellent sport bike with a strong engine, excellent handling characteristics, and a full fairing. This was Kawasaki's 1984 magazine ad announcing "The next generation of Kawasaki performance." *Copyright © 2000 Kawasaki Motor Corps. USA*

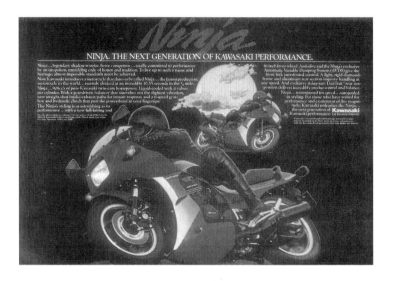

surgetank/airbox and then into the engine. Fuel delivery occurred just prior to the air going into the engine and was handled by Kawasaki's Digital Fuel Injection (DFI). Altogether a very complicated system with many things to go wrong. The system did have one positive effect: the engine was rated at 112 horsepower at 8,000 rpm.

Production of this power was dependent on the turbocharger and one of its unpleasant side effects, turbo lag. Turbo lag was the delay between when the throttle was opened and when the engine started making serious power. This delay was due to the time required for the turbocharger impeller to spin up and start delivering boost to the engine. In a straight line, this was more an interesting side effect of the turbocharger than anything serious. In tight, curvy roads, though, it could be very interesting. While the 750 Turbo was stable in a straight line, curvy roads required some finesse with the throttle. Open the throttle too much in a turn without accounting for the turbo lag and you could find yourself in a difficult situation with the engine suddenly making more power than you had expected.

Beyond the turbocharger and the interesting handling were the looks of the bike. The 750 Turbo had a nicely shaped full sport fairing and came in a beautiful red and black paint scheme. Even the inner part of the wheel rims and spokes were red. Compared to the other factory turbos, the Kawasaki was much more complete looking. Even the Suzuki XN85, with its Katana-based styling, did not look as good.

The Kawasaki 750 Turbo, like all the factory turbos, is a very collectible bike. Add to this that the Kawasaki 750 was the fastest of the factory turbos and was only available for two years and you have a very desirable, if rather scarce, motorcycle. As you would with all of the turbocharged bikes, be sure that the turbocharger and all the related parts and assemblies are functioning properly. With the Kawasaki, also be sure the digital fuel-injection system is fully functional. These parts are all very expensive to replace. If you are unfamiliar with how to check the operation of the turbocharger and the fuel injection, it will be worthwhile to have someone familiar with these systems check them out for you.

Future collectibles
1984–1986, ZX900 Ninja (908 cc)

Collectibility	★★
Passenger Accommodations	★★ 1/2
Reliability	★★★★
Parts/Service Availability	★★★★
Handling	★★★★★
Engine Performance	★★★★ 1/2

Engine	four cylinder, liquid cooled four-stroke, DOHC four valve head
Bore & stroke	72.5x55.0 mm
Displacement	908 cc
Compression ratio	11.0:1
Bhp at rpm	115 at 9,500
Transmission	6 speed
Primary drive	straight cut gears
Clutch	multi disc, wet plate
Brakes: front	dual disc
Brakes: rear	single disc
Tire size: front	120/80V16
Tire size: rear	130/80V18
Fuel capacity	5.8 gal
Wheelbase	58.8 in.
Weight	565 lb
Seat height	30.5 in.
Quarter-mile	10.96 sec at 122.3 mph*
Top Speed	153.9 mph*

*Motorcyclist magazine test, August 1984

For Kawasaki, the 900 Ninja was the bike in which all the different elements of the sport bike came together and worked as they were intended. Previous bikes like the ELR and the Turbo had come close, but the ELR was a limited-production model and the Turbo was, well, a turbo. The 900 Ninja had a powerful engine, excellent handling, and a full sport fairing for the correct look.

There were no technological breakthroughs in the 900 Ninja engine, but it did have interesting features for a Kawasaki engine. The engine was a liquid-cooled inline four, with four valves per cylinder. The four-valve head was significant since it was Kawasaki's first, even though four-valve heads were in common use by other manufacturers. The engine also had a counterbalancer shaft mounted in front of the crankshaft that was gear driven from the crankshaft. Also different from standard Kawasaki practice was the mounting of the alternator behind the cylinders rather than on the end of the crankshaft. Mounting it this way reduced engine width. The transmission was a six-speed and the clutch was hydraulically actuated.

The bike is a 1986 600 Ninja, not much different than the first year 1985 model. The full fairing and red and black paint scheme suit my taste perfectly. When I see the bike, I remember the moment in 1986 when I went into a Kawasaki shop and saw a similar 600 Ninja. I knew immediately that the Ninja was a bike that I must own.

I push the starter button and the bike starts right up. It strikes me that by the mid-1980s, motorcycles had become quite advanced technically. No more kick-starting, no wondering if you were going to foul a plug before the trip was over. There is no doubt that motorcycle technology has continued to progress since then, but the bike I'm looking at is quite sophisticated. I'm sure that someone 20 years old would not view the 600 Ninja as being as technically advanced as I do. I guess it depends on where in time your frame of reference starts.

I get on the bike and head for a nearby section of twisty back road. The throttle response is good and the acceleration is very brisk. The road gets curvy and I start to enjoy how things are going. The bike handles well and is very confidence-inspiring. I pick up the pace and am still pleased with the way everything feels. This is definitely different than my experience riding an early H2 over this same type of road. The Ninja is certainly a very entertaining bike on the twisty roads. I decide it's time to try the bike out where more speed is possible, so I head for the highway.

Getting onto the highway, I go down around an entrance ramp that I've been on many times before. The ramp is freshly paved and very smooth. There is no traffic so I decide to see what happens when I get near the handling limit on this bike. I lean it over and roll on the throttle. I finally reach a point where I sense that both wheels are starting to slip. Nothing abrupt, just a very slight, controllable slip. I enter the highway and am pleased to see that there is not a single vehicle in sight. I twist the throttle open and accelerate. My speed rises quickly. Yes, there are bikes that are faster

Where the 900 Ninja really excelled was in handling. The rear suspension was Kawasaki's rising rate, single-shock Uni-track setup. The front forks had 38-millimeter fork tubes that were the largest that Kawasaki had used up to this time on a sport bike. The front suspension also included Kawasaki's Automatic Variable Damping System (AVDS) anti-dive front fork. The total suspension package worked very well and the 900 Ninja was considered to be one of the best handling bikes of the time, excellent on tight back roads but also very stable in high-speed corners.

The 900 Ninja wasn't the fastest motorcycle in 1984, but it was one of the most well-rounded. It did everything very well and was considered by many people the best sport bike of the time. The 900 Ninja was the start of a long line of Kawasaki sport bikes that over the years have been produced in many variations. Currently the early 900 Ninjas are still very reasonably priced, available, and an excellent bet as a future collectible. When looking at a Ninja for purchase, besides checking out the mechanical condition, be sure to check the condition of the fairing and other cosmetic parts.

1985–1997, ZX600 Ninja (592 cc)

Collectibility	★★
Passenger Accommodations	★★
Reliability	★★★★
Parts/Service Availability	★★★★
Handling	★★★★★
Engine Performance	★★★★

Engine	four cylinder, liquid cooled four-stroke, DOHC four valve head
Bore & stroke	60.0x52.4 mm
Displacement	592 cc
Compression ratio	11.0:1
Bhp at rpm	75 at 10,500
Transmission	6 speed
Primary drive	chain
Clutch	multi disc, wet plate
Brakes: front	dual disc
Brakes: rear	single disc
Tire size: front	120/90V16
Tire size: rear	130/90V16
Fuel capacity	4.3 gal
Wheelbase	56.3 in.
Weight	472 lb
Seat height	30.5 in.
Quarter-mile	12.06 sec at 111.3 mph*
Top Speed	153.9 mph*

*Motorcyclist magazine test, January 1985

In the early 1980s, Kawasaki had dominated the mid-displacement sporting bike class with the GPz550. By 1984, the Honda 500 Interceptor and the Yamaha FJ600 had come onto the scene and it was time for Kawasaki to come up with something new to reestablish its position at the top of the class. With the 600 Ninja, Kawasaki definitely attained this goal.

The 600 Ninja followed the theme that had been set by the 900 Ninja, a nice engine with plenty of power, excellent handling, and a very stylish full sport fairing. The engine, like the bigger Ninja, had four valves per cylinder and was liquid cooled. The transmission was also similar, having six speeds. The 600 Ninja engine produced 75 horsepower at 10,500 rpm; 10 horsepower more than the GPz550 engine produced.

The suspension setup was also like the bigger Ninja. The rear suspension was Kawasaki's Uni-trak setup and the front suspension had what was, for the time, large 37-millimeter fork tubes with the AVDS anti-dive system. The two Ninjas differed in their frame design, with the 600 Ninja using a perimeter frame. The overall effect, though, was very much like the 900 Ninja, only in a smaller, lighter package. The 600 Ninja was fast and handled very well in all circumstances.

At this time, the 600 Ninja is still just a used bike. As nice as they were, they did not have the pizzaz or the limited production to become an instant collectible. For the enthusiast interested in 1980s sport bikes or the collector of Kawasakis, the 600 Ninja is a very interesting and available motorcycle that will increase in desirability as time goes on. As with the larger Ninjas, attention should be paid to the fairing and other cosmetic pieces when buying a 600 Ninja.

and yes, you have to keep the revs up because of the engine's size, but there is no doubt that this is a fast bike. I quickly reach the edge of my comfort zone and the bike is still accelerating. I hastily look at the instruments and see that the tach has just passed redline and simultaneously realize that I still have another gear to go. I shift up to sixth, let out the clutch, and again start accelerating. I quickly realize that as fast as I am going and knowing what's up ahead, I'm going to have to shut it down very soon. I back off the throttle and catch my breath. It's been less than a minute since I started down the entrance ramp, but it's a slice of time that I don't think I'll ever forget. I take the next exit and head back to where I started my ride.

Continuing at a more leisurely pace, I start thinking about the way I am sitting on the bike. The seating position is something I have mixed emotions about. When I'm riding the bike quickly on a winding back road or at extra-legal speeds on the highway, the riding position feels natural and makes me feel very attuned to what the bike is doing. When the traffic gets tight and there are a lot of traffic lights to deal with, the riding position becomes less comfortable. I guess that considering what the Ninja is made for, this is really not a dilemma. If you want to go for a leisurely cruise or parading for the ladies, the 600 Ninja is not your bike. If you want to go for a fast ride and have fun doing it, the Ninja is an excellent selection.

The ZX600 Ninja had superb looks and excellent performance.
Copyright © 2000 Kawasaki Motor Corps. USA

Suzuki

MODELS COVERED

T20 X6 Hustler	GT750	GSX-R750
X5 Invader	GT380	GS850
T500 Titan	GT550	GS1000/GS1000S
T-125 Stinger	RE5	GS1000SZ
MT50 Trail Hopper	GS750	XN85 Turbo

Suzuki was founded in 1909 by Michio Suzuki in Hamamatsu, Japan, to build textile-weaving looms. The company successfully built looms for the next several decades, and in 1937, the decision was made to supplement the business by building automobiles. Significantly, a Suzuki four-cylinder, four-stroke, liquid-cooled engine powered these early Suzuki automobiles. With the onset of the World War II, Suzuki was ordered by the Japanese government to cease the frivolous production of automobiles and for the duration of

The 1966 X6 was an exciting motorcycle. With its six-speed transmission and impressive performance it made a definite impression on motorcyclists of the time. *Steve Lindley*

the war, Suzuki, like many manufacturers, produced needed material to support the Japanese war effort.

At the end of the war, Suzuki resumed the manufacture of looms but not automobiles. At the time, the future of the loom business looked promising, but due to the financial situation in Japan and other business factors, it was a very volatile and unpredictable business. By 1951, conditions didn't favor loom production. The state of the Japanese economy and the general lack of inexpensive transportation meant that conditions were ripe for Suzuki to once again enter the transportation manufacturing business.

The first product for the company in this new endeavor was the Power Free. The Power Free was a bicycle with a 36 cc two-stroke engine attached to it. The Power Free had an interesting feature that allowed the rider to choose between engine power, pedal power, or both. The mechanism that gave the rider this choice of power modes was innovative enough that the Japanese Patent Office gave Suzuki a subsidy to continue motorcycle development. Shortly after the Power Free came the 60 cc Diamond Free, which, like the Power Free, was a bicycle with an engine attached to it.

In 1954, Suzuki introduced its next model, the 90 cc single-cylinder, four-stroke powered Colleda. The Colleda was Suzuki's first complete motorcycle. By this time, Suzuki was firmly into the two-wheeled transportation business, producing 6,000 units per month. As was fitting for a successful motorcycle manufacturer, the company name was changed to Suzuki Motor Co. Ltd.

Over the next few years, development of new models continued, with 125 cc and 250 cc models joining the lineup. By 1962, Suzuki was the number-two Japanese manufacturer of motorcycles, second only to Honda.

In 1963, Suzuki decided to broaden its market and began export to Europe, Australia, and the United States. U.S. Suzuki Motor Corp. established an office in Los Angeles and sales of Suzuki motorcycles started in the United States. At this point, Honda and Yamaha, as well as the soon-to-disappear Tohatsu and Lilac, were already in the U.S. market. Suzuki, the second-largest motorcycle manufacturer in the world, was sure that it could compete in the U.S. market. Motorcycle sales over the next 30-plus years would prove that it was right.

A rear shot of the X6 showing its sleek lines and the Suzuki logo on the back of the seat. *Steve Lindley*

A Suzuki ad for the T20 X6 extols its performance and shows many of the features of the bike. *Suzuki Motor Corp., U.S.A.*

1966–1968, X6 Hustler (247 cc)

Collectibility	★★★ 1/2
Passenger Accommodations	★★
Reliability	★★★
Parts/Service Availability	★★★
Handling	★★ 1/2
Engine Performance	★★ 1/2

Engine	twin cylinder, piston port, two-stroke
Bore & stroke	54x54 mm
Displacement	247 cc
Compression ratio	7.3:1
Bhp at rpm	29 at 7,500
Transmission	6 speed
Primary drive	helical gear
Clutch	multi disc, wet plate
Brakes: front	twin-leading-shoe drum
Brakes: rear	single-leading-shoe drum
Tire size: front	2.75-18
Tire size: rear	3.00-18
Fuel capacity	3.7gal
Wheelbase	50.6 in.
Weight	301 lb
Seat height	30.8 in.
Quarter-mile	15.3 sec at 84 mph*
Top Speed	92 mph*

Cycle World magazine test, October 1965

The X6 was a significant step in the establishment of Suzuki as an innovative manufacturer of performance-oriented motorcycles. Prior to the X6, Suzukis were known as reliable, well-made motorcycles. The X6 was not only reliable and well made, but also it was fast, and handled and stopped well. The performance of the X6 added a new facet to Suzuki's reputation.

The engine in the X6 was a piston-port 250 cc two-stroke producing 29 horsepower. Lubrication was by Suzuki's Posiforce lubrication system, so premixing of gas and oil for the engine was unnecessary. The engine transmitted its power to the rear wheel through a six-speed transmission. Today, six-speed transmissions are viewed as commonplace, but in the 1960s, six-speed transmissions were only used in factory racers. The six-speed transmission in the X6 was a significant innovation for a street bike and served as the inspiration for the X6's name.

With its two-stroke engine and six-speed transmission, the X6's acceleration was excellent. Quarter-mile times were a little over 15 seconds. The six-speed also provided the right gear for every situation. For fast riding on a twisty road, the X6 had a gear available to keep the engine in the power band, and for highway riding, sixth gear was available for comfortable cruising.

In addition to six speeds, the transmission also had another feature that was innovative for its time. When downshifted from second gear, the transmission would shift into neutral. A second push on the shift lever was required to shift into first gear. This allowed neutral to be found very easily when pulling up to a stop. When shifting up through the gears, the transmission shifted directly from first to second.

The X6 also had an interesting fuel gauge. At the left front of the gas tank was a clear tube that connected to both the bottom and the top of the gas tank. The tube allowed the rider to see how much gas was in the tank. While perhaps a little crude in its application, it was still certainly effective. This feature was used on other Suzukis of the time, and it was one of the more endearing features of the X6.

The X6, also referred to as the T20, was the first Suzuki to really make an impression on the U.S. market. It had style, performance, and a six-speed transmission. Although they are rather difficult to find, if you want an example of one of Suzuki's early performance-oriented motorcycles, the X6 is the bike to have. When buying an X6, besides making sure that the motorcycle is in good mechanical condition, check to see that the gas tank, tank emblems, and exhaust are all in good condition with no chips, scratches, or dents.

1967, X5 Invader (196 cc)

Collectibility	★★★
Passenger Accommodations	★★
Reliability	★★★
Parts/Service Availability	★★
Handling	★★ 1/2
Engine Performance	★★

Engine	twin cylinder, piston port, two-stroke
Bore & stroke	50x50 mm
Displacement	196 cc
Compression ratio	7:1
Bhp at rpm	23 at 7,500
Transmission	5 speed
Primary drive	gear
Clutch	multi disc, wet plate
Brakes: front	twin-leading-shoe drum
Brakes: rear	single-leading-shoe drum
Tire size: front	2.75-18
Tire size: rear	2.75-18
Fuel capacity	3.6 gal
Wheelbase	50.0 in
Weight	272 lb
Seat height	30.7 in.
Quarter-mile	17.4 sec at 76 mph*
Top Speed	88 mph*

*Cycle World magazine test, May 1967

The X5 Invader was very much like the X6, only in a smaller package and with one fewer gear in the transmission. *Suzuki Motor Corp., U.S.A.*

This is a late X5. Note the different tank shape, tank badges, seat, and turn signals. I love the styling of both the bike and the model. *Suzuki Motor Corp., U.S.A.*

The T500 Titan was a significant step forward for two-stroke engine technology when it was introduced in 1967. The bike was fast and good looking, a winning combination. This is a 1972 Titan. *Suzuki Motor Corp., U.S.A.*

Very similar in appearance and closely related to the X6 was the X5 Invader. The X5 had a 200 cc engine and a five-speed transmission. The only other feature missing from the very successful X6 package was the tachometer, which was available as an option. With the smaller engine, 20 percent less horsepower, and only five speeds in the transmission, the X5 did not have the acceleration of the X6. Top speed of the X5, however, was reasonably close to the top speed of the X6.

The X5 did have a feature that would eventually become common that was not found on the X6 or any other motorcycles at the time. The fuel petcock was vacuum actuated by a rubber hose connected to the left intake manifold. When the engine was running, the vacuum in the intake manifold opened the petcock.

While not as collectible as an X6, the X5 is still a very interesting mid-1960s Suzuki. The styling and the two-stroke engine are very appealing, and the X5 is certainly a bike that is not often seen. Checking out an X5 for purchase is much like an X6 except that extra attention needs to be paid to all items since X5 parts are even harder to find than X6 parts.

1967–1977, T500 Titan (492 cc)

Collectibility	★★★ 1/2
Passenger Accommodations	★★★
Reliability	★★★
Parts/Service Availability	★★★
Handling	★★★
Engine Performance	★★★

Engine	twin cylinder, piston port, two-stroke
Bore & stroke	70x64 mm
Displacement	492 cc
Compression ratio	6.6:1
Bhp at rpm	46 at 7,000
Transmission	5 speed
Primary drive	gear
Clutch	multi disc, wet plate
Brakes: front	twin-leading-shoe drum
Brakes: rear	single-leading-shoe drum
Tire size: front	3.25-19
Tire size: rear	3.50-18
Fuel capacity	3.7 gal
Wheelbase	52.7 in.
Weight	391 lb
Seat height	32.3 in.
Quarter-mile	14.1 sec at 94 mph*
Top Speed	109 mph*

Cycle World magazine test, December 1967

After its initial role as Suzuki's near Superbike the Titan became Suzuki's high value middleweight. Styling was changed but the basic design stayed the same for most of the Titan's life. While most of the Suzuki line had disc brakes in 1973 the Titan still had drum brakes, as seen on this 1974 model. It was 1976 before the Titan was available with disc brakes. *Suzuki Motor Corp., U.S.A.*

The most significant aspect of the twin-cylinder T500 was its 500 cc two-stroke engine. Until the introduction of the T500, it was considered impossible to build a reliable two-stroke engine with a displacement of much over 350 cc. It was firmly believed that two-stroke engines as large as the T500s were sure to overheat and seize. The T500 firmly dispelled this myth.

With the 500 cc two-stroke engine came very impressive acceleration. The quarter-mile time for the T500 was just over 14 seconds and the top speed was about 110 miles per hour. In addition to the performance, the engine proved to be very reliable.

Handling, on the other hand, was not very good for the first T500s. Noted problems were wobbling and a front suspension that would bottom out under extreme conditions. These problems were corrected on later versions of the bike.

Styling on the T500 was definitely late 1960s, with lines very similar to the X6. The chrome tank side panels and the exhaust running parallel to the ground were very attractive and definitely of the era. There were also items that were indicative of coming styling trends. The gauges on the T500 were not mounted in the top of the headlight, as were most gauges at the time. Instead, the tachometer and speedometer were individual gauges, each in its own separate housing.

Even after the introduction of many larger and faster bikes, the T500 remained in production up to the 1977 GT500. The styling was updated, improvements were made, and eventually a disc brake was added, but the bike remained basically the same over its production life. The T500 represented good value for the money. Performance on later models, while no longer cutting edge, was still very acceptable, and over the long term the bike proved very reliable. The T500 was definitely a success for Suzuki.

The T500 was one of the first Superbikes, or at the very least the direct predecessor to the Superbikes. For a short period of time it was the king, but it wasn't long before the two first undisputed Superbikes, the Honda CB750 and the Kawasaki Mach III, were to come onto the scene. The T500s, particularly the first ones, are very desirable bikes and can require a fair amount of searching to find. The later bikes, while not as collectible, still require consideration as examples of late 1960s Suzuki two-stroke technology. When purchasing a T500, look for a bike with a good, original exhaust and a clean, undented gas tank. These items, as with most bikes, are difficult to replace.

Suzuki Model Year Designators

Suzuki model designations are clearer than most of the other manufacturers' about indicating what a particular model's displacement is. While prior to the 1970s the model designation did not always clearly indicate the displacement, as with the K11 or the T20, by the 1970s a model's displacement was much more obvious. A Suzuki T350 is obviously a 350 cc machine, whereas it is not so clear that a Yamaha R5 is a 350 cc machine or a Honda CBX is a 1,000 cc.

There is a part of the Suzuki model designation that is not quite as clear in its meaning. This is the alpha character at the end of the model designation. While it is fairly obvious that a GT750K is different than a GT750M, it is not readily apparent what the difference is. Suzuki used this alpha character as part of its model designation to identify the model year beginning in 1971. Thus a GT750K is a 1973 GT750 and a GT750M is a 1975 GT750.

The alpha designation should always match the model year. A Suzuki model available in the 1970s with an M at the end is always a 1975 model-year bike.

This is a list of model-year designators for 1971 through 1989.

R	1971	X	1981
J	1972	Z	1982
K	1973	D	1983
L	1974	E	1984
M	1975	F	1985
A	1976	G	1986
B	1977	H	1987
C	1978	J	1988
N	1979	K	1989
T	1980		

Right: The TS125 Stinger had interesting styling, with its long sleek gas tank, high-level exhaust with shiny stingers, and almost horizontal engine cylinders. This is a 1970 model with the medal Suzuki tank badges. *David Paryzek*

A close-up view of the TS125 engine with its down draft carburetors. *David Paryzek*

Seen from the rear, the TS125 is as attractive as it is from the side. *David Paryzek*

1969–1970, T125 Stinger (125 cc)

Collectibility	★★★
Passenger Accommodations	★
Reliability	★★★
Parts/Service Availability	★★ 1/2
Handling	★★
Engine Performance	★ 1/2

Engine	twin cylinder, piston port, two-stroke
Bore & stroke	43x43 mm
Displacement	125 cc
Compression ratio	7.3:1
Bhp at rpm	15.1 at 8,500
Transmission	5 speed
Primary drive	n/a
Clutch	multi disc, wet plate
Brakes: front	single-leading-shoe drum
Brakes: rear	single-leading-shoe drum
Tire size: front	2.50-18
Tire size: rear	2.75-18
Fuel capacity	1.9 gal
Wheelbase	46.9 in.
Weight	206 lb dry
Seat height	n/a
Eighth-mile	11.3 sec*
Top Speed	75 mph*

*Suzuki sales brochure

The Stinger was a 125 cc twin-cylinder two-stroke with dazzling looks and a rather unusual engine configuration, which added to its appeal. The engine is a twin-cylinder, with the cylinders positioned almost horizontally. To accommodate the horizontal cylinders, downdraft carburetors were used. Performance from the 125 cc engine was quite good and the bike had a reputation for being very entertaining to ride.

The look of the horizontal cylinders was complemented by the high-level exhaust. The pipes came out of the bottom of the cylinders, turned up along the outside of the cylinders, passed just above them, then turned back to enter into the long, slim mufflers that end just behind the rear tire. To complete the alluring appearance, the gas tank was long and slender and the seat had a turned-up tail. The whole look of the T125 was very striking.

With its interesting looks and peppy performance, the Stinger appeals to the collector of small displacement bikes looking for something a bit unusual. T125s are not very common, and some searching will be required if you need one for your collection. The exhaust should be in good condition on any Stinger being considered for purchase.

1971–1973, MT50 Trailhopper (49 cc)

Collectibility	★★
Passenger Accommodations	★★★
Reliability	★★★
Parts/Service Availability	★
Handling	★
Engine Performance	★

The MT50 Trailhopper was Suzuki's entry to the mini-bike war of the early 1970s. The Trailhopper had an interesting appearance that looked quite different from other mini-bikes of the time. Interestingly, the front "porthole" in the tank cover contains the ignition key. *Amy Douvlos*

Engine	single cylinder, reed valve, two-stroke
Bore & stroke	41x28 mm
Displacement	49 cc
Compression ratio	6.9:1
Bhp at rpm	3 at 6,000
Transmission	3 speed,
Primary drive	n/a
Clutch	multi disc, wet plate, automatic, centrifugal
Brakes: front	single-leading-shoe drum
Brakes: rear	single-leading-shoe drum
Tire size: front	3.50-8
Tire size: rear	3.50-8
Fuel capacity	0.65 gal
Wheelbase	37 in.
Weight	132 lb
Seat height	n/a
Quarter-mile	n/a
Top Speed	n/a

The front fender of the MT50 displayed a very stylish Trailhopper sticker. Also seen on both sides of the forks are the knobs that secured the folding handlebars. *Amy Douvlos*

Suzuki's late entry into the mini-bike market came with the MT50's introduction in 1971. The Trailhopper's engine was a 50 cc three-horsepower, reed-valve, single-cylinder two-stroke with a three-speed transmission and an automatic centrifugal clutch. The bike was small, had folding handlebars, and was fairly light at 132 pounds. It could be carried in the back of a car or van, making it good portable transportation.

The Trailhopper was similar in specification to many of the mini-bikes available in the early 1970s. Like the Trailhopper, the Honda Z50 and the Kawasaki MT1 also had folding handlebars, chunky tires, and a three-speed transmission with an automatic clutch.

What made the Trailhopper stand out was its unusual looks. The Honda and the Kawasaki both looked like small motorcycles with a separate gas tank, a seat attached to the frame, and an exposed exhaust system. The MT1, on the other hand, had a covering that ran from the front of the frame back to the rear shock mounts. This covering went over the gas tank, covered the high-level exhaust, and went under the seat. The seat itself was on a pillar like a bicycle seat and was adjustable to three levels of height. All this gave the MT50 a very distinct, futuristic appearance.

The MT50, in direct contrast to the Honda Z50, was only in production for three years. Due to this short production run, there are not a lot of MT50s around. If you come across one, it is well worth having just for its looks alone. MT50s are rather rare and any bike being looked at should be checked to be sure that as many parts as possible are correct and original since MT50 parts can be hard to find.

As with many mini-bikes the Trailhopper could be reconfigured for easy transportation. Here the seat side cover and mirror have been removed and the handlebars folded back for easy storage. *Amy Douvlos*

1972–1977, GT750 LeMans (739 cc) "Water Buffalo"

Collectibility	★★★★
Passenger Accommodations	★★★★
Reliability	★★★★
Parts/Service Availability	★★★ 1/2
Handling	★★★
Engine Performance	★★★ 1/2

Due to its liquid cooling, the appearance of the GT750 was unique, with a radiator mounted in front of the engine and no fins on the engine cylinders.
Tom Leonard, owner

Engine	three cylinder, piston port two-stroke, liquid cooled
Bore & stroke	70x64 mm
Displacement	739 cc
Compression ratio	6.7:1
Bhp at rpm	67 at 6,500
Transmission	5 speed
Primary drive	helical gear
Clutch	multi disc, wet plate
Brakes: front	four-leading shoe drum
Brakes: rear	single-leading shoe drum
Tire size: front	3.25-19
Tire size: rear	4.00-18
Fuel capacity	4.5 gal
Wheelbase	58 in.
Weight	524 lb
Seat height	32.0 in.
Quarter-mile	13.87 sec at 93.55 mph*
Top Speed	107 mph*

* *Cycle World* magazine test, December 1971

The front brake on the 1972 GT750 worked great and was beautiful to look at. The GT750 drum brake setup is now very much in demand among vintage racing enthusiasts.
Tom Leonard, owner

In 1972, with the introduction of the GT750, affectionately known by many as the Water Buffalo, Suzuki finally had its first indisputable Superbike. All of the necessary ingredients were present that had been missing from the T500. The GT750 had a powerful, large-displacement multi-cylinder engine, it offered technical innovation, it had performance, and it had eye-catching looks.

The engine in the GT750 was a 750 cc two-stroke three-cylinder. In 1972, the GT750 was not the only 750 cc two-stroke triple on the market (the Kawasaki H2 was also introduced in 1972) but it did make use of a technical innovation that would become common over the next 20 years—liquid-cooling. Although Suzuki was not the first to build a liquid-cooled motorcycle (Scott was building liquid-cooled two-strokes in the 1920s) the technique was not being used

The introduction of the 1972 GT750, with its large displacement water-cooled engine, gave Suzuki a true Superbike. The 1972 GT750 was fast and had a great four\ leading shoe front brake. *Tom Leonard, owner*

The rear of the GT750, showing the "Suzuki GT" script on the rear of the seat and the unusual three-into-four exhaust system. *Tom Leonard, owner*

in production motorcycles in the early 1970s. In addition to the liquid-cooling, the engine was rated at 67 horsepower and gave the Suzuki impressive, if not earth-shattering, performance. Braking was excellent with the four-leading-shoe drum brakes, which were made even better when upgraded to disc. With the liquid-cooled engine, Suzuki had two of the pieces for the GT750 to qualify as a Superbike.

The GT750's appearance was the third part of the Superbike formula. The eye-catching attractive looks of the bike were due to several different factors. First was the size of the GT750. It was an impressively large bike. Then there were the three-cylinder finless engine and the exhaust system. The three-cylinder engine led Suzuki to use an interesting three-into-four exhaust system. The left cylinder fed into a pipe on the left and the right cylinder fed into a pipe on the right but the center cylinder exhaust pipe split into two smaller pipes with one on each side of the bike running under the larger pipes from the outside cylinders. This gave the GT750 a symmetrical appearance from the rear that was not seen on the Kawasaki triples, which used one pipe on the left and two on the right for its three-cylinder exhaust systems. The other eye-catching piece to the GT750's looks was the radiator, which was positioned in front of the engine. This added a unique appearance to the bike when viewed from the front.

The GT750 remained in production until 1977 and went through several modifications and improvements over the years. In 1973 dual front disc brakes replaced the twin-leading-shoe drum brake, and in 1974 a digital gear indicator was added. It's also interesting to note that while the Kawasaki triples were toned down and lost performance over the production run, the last GT750s produced more power and were faster than the earlier GT750s.

The GT750 is a significant bike in the development of larger displacement Suzukis. It was Suzuki's flagship model during the mid-1970s and carried Suzuki through the RE5 episode. The GT750 is a perfect bike for someone looking for a large, reliable two-stroke who wants something a bit more refined than a Kawasaki H2. While the GT750 is not a particularly rare bike, it certainly has the reputation and unique looks to attract attention on the street or at a vintage motorcycle meet. When evaluating a GT750 for purchase, be sure that the exhaust is correct and in good condition. If buying a 1972 model, be sure the front brakes are the correct four-leading-shoe drum assembly.

Over the GT750 production run, the performance of the bike got better each year. This is a 1975 GT750 with its high performance engine and twin discs front brake. *Andrew Brothers*

1972–1977, GT380 Sebring (371 cc)

Collectibility	★★★
Passenger Accommodations	★★ 1/2
Reliability	★★★ 1/2
Parts/Service Availability	★★★
Handling	★★★
Engine Performance	★★ 1/2

Engine	three cylinder, piston port two-stroke
Bore & stroke	54 x54 mm
Displacement	371 cc
Compression ratio	6.7:1
Bhp at rpm	38 at 7,500
Transmission	6 speed
Primary drive	gear
Clutch	multi disc, wet plate
Brakes: front	twin-leading shoe, drum
Brakes: rear	single-leading shoe, drum
Tire size: front	3.00-19
Tire size: rear	3.50-18
Fuel capacity	4.0 gal
Wheelbase	55 in.
Weight	392 lb
Seat height	31.25 in.
Quarter-mile	14.58 sec at 87.97 mph*
Top Speed	98.36 mph*

* *Cycle World* magazine test, June 1972

The extensive GT750 instrument cluster included not only the typical speedometer, tachometer, and warning lights but also included a temperature gauge and a gear position indicator. The filler cap for the radiator was under a cover at the front of the gas tank. The cover has been raised for the photo. A very similar set of instruments and radiator filler were used on the 1976 RE5. *Andrew Brothers*

The GT380 was the second and smallest version of Suzuki's new three-cylinder two-stroke engine family. Many features of the GT380 were the same as the GT750, but on a smaller scale. The GT380 shared the same three-cylinder engine configuration and the same distinctive three-into-four exhaust system. One of the particular differences between the two bikes, though, was that the GT380 was air-cooled, rather than liquid-cooled.

Being air-cooled, the GT380 employed the Ram Air system, used on Suzuki's racers, to improve cooling efficiency. Ram Air was an air scoop that

The 1972 GT380 was the smallest of Suzuki's very successful three-cylinder two-stroke line. Although similar in many ways to the GT750, it differed in that it was air cooled and used Suzuki's Ram Air system to increase cooling efficiency. *Steve Lindley*

A view of the front of the GT380's engine, showing the Ram Air cylinder head and scoop. *Steve Lindley*

went over the top of the fins on the cylinder head. The scoop improved the airflow over the cylinder head and thus improved cylinder head cooling. With the improved cooling, the engine did not experience the power loss typical of a two-stroke as the engine heated up. The Ram Air scoop also added a distinctive look to the engines that were equipped with it.

Handling, for the GT380, was reported to be very good, with no wobble in the corners and no need for a steering damper. As was common with a lot of bikes at this time, the GT380 did have a few pieces that would contact the pavement when the bike was driven hard through the corners. In the GT380's case the center stand was the first thing to hit during brisk riding.

The GT380 remained in production until 1977 and was the last of the two-stroke Suzuki street bikes. Although not as technically innovative as the GT750, the GT380 is an excellent choice for someone looking for a mid-to-late 1970s Suzuki two-stroke. One can usually be located with a moderate amount of searching. When buying a GT380, look for the normal things; a good, sound exhaust system; and unblemished cosmetics.

This is a 1974 GT380 with a single disc front brake. *Suzuki Motor Corp., U.S.A.*

1972–1977, GT550 Indy (543 cc)

Collectibility	★★★
Passenger Accommodations	★★★
Reliability	★★★ 1/2
Parts/Service Availability	★★★
Handling	★★★
Engine Performance	★★★

Engine	three cylinder, piston port two-stroke
Bore & stroke	61x62 mm
Displacement	543 cc
Compression ratio	6.7:1
Bhp at rpm	50 at 6,500
Transmission	5 speed
Primary drive	gear
Clutch	multi disc, wet plate
Brakes: front	twin-leading-shoe drum
Brakes: rear	single-leading-shoe drum
Tire size: front	3.25-19
Tire size: rear	4.00-18
Fuel capacity	4.0 gal
Wheelbase	57.5 in.
Weight	472 lb
Seat height	31.5 in.
Quarter-mile	14.59 sec at 87.8 mph*
Top Speed	98 mph*

* *Cycle World* magazine test, January 1973

The GT550 was the third of the Suzuki Triples and was also introduced in 1972. It rounded out the lineup by being smaller, less complex, less expensive, and somewhat slower than the GT750 but bigger and—due to its larger displacement—more powerful than the GT380.

The GT550 also presented a distinct alternative to potential buyers looking for a bike in the 500 cc class. In 1972, for those not interested in the four-stroke Honda CB500, there were really only two choices, the Kawasaki Mach III or the GT550. While the Kawasaki had excellent straight-line acceleration, it also had a peaky power curve and could be a real handful to ride. For the street racers there was only one choice, the Mach III. For all the other riders there was the GT550.

The engine and most other features of the GT550 were very similar to those of the GT380.

The three-cylinder GT550 fit nicely in Suzuki's lineup between the GT380 and the GT750. This is a 1972 GT550 with the front drum brake, and again showing the Ram Air cooling. *Suzuki Motor Corp., U.S.A.*

The air-cooled, three-cylinder two-stroke engine configuration with Ram Air was used on both bikes. The brakes on both for the first year were drums and the styling of both was very similar. The main differences between the GT550 and the GT380 were that the GT550 had the extra displacement, was physically larger, weighed approximately 50 pounds more, and had a five-speed rather than a six-speed transmission.

The GT550 was in production from 1972 through 1977 and shares the same development trends and changes as the GT750 and the GT380. Disc brakes were added in 1973 with a single disc configuration for the front end as on the GT380.

In 1973 the GT550, like most of the Suzuki line, came with a front disc brake. *Andrew Brothers*

Engine development continued during the life of the bike and the engine developed three more horsepower in 1975 than it did in 1972.

The GT550 is another example of Suzuki's three-cylinder two-stroke technology in the early 1970s. For the present-day collector, the GT550 presents much the same alternative it did when it was new, a bike simpler than a GT750, bigger than a GT380, and a clear alternative to a Kawasaki Mach III. Like the GT380, GT550s can usually be located with a moderate amount of searching. As you would with the GT380, be sure that the exhaust and all cosmetics are in good condition when evaluating a GT550 for purchase.

The left side of the GT550, showing the Ram Air system. The four-pipe exhaust system, with its two smaller pipes for the center cylinder, can be seen with the right side pipes visible through the rear wheel. *Andrew Brothers*

1975–1976, RE5 (497 cc)

Collectibility	★★★★
Passenger Accommodations	★★★★
Reliability	★★★★ 1/2
Parts/Service Availability	★★
Handling	★★★ 1/2
Engine Performance	★★★

Engine	single rotor, Wankel rotary, liquid cooled
Radius, width, eccentricity	102x66.55x14 mm
Displacement	497 cc
Compression ratio	9.4:1
Bhp at rpm	62 at 6,500
Transmission	5 speed
Primary drive	duplex chain
Clutch	multi disc, wet plate
Brakes: front	twin disc
Brakes: rear	single-leading shoe, drum
Tire size: front	3.25-19
Tire size: rear	4.00-18
Fuel capacity	4.5 gal
Wheelbase	59.1 in.
Weight	617 lb
Seat height	n/a
Quarter-mile	14.78 sec at 87.04 mph*
Top Speed	102 mph*

* *Cycle World* magazine test, September 1975

By the mid-1970s, the Wankel engine, commonly referred to as the rotary engine, was thought by many to be the internal-combustion engine that offered the most promise for future development. Since the rotary had fewer moving parts, some thought that it would eventually replace both the two-stroke and four-stroke piston engines as the engine of choice for cars and motorcycles. There were definitely problems to be solved with things like the rotary's tip seals and its large appetite for fuel, but the Mazda RX-2 and RX-3 automobiles were proof that rotary engines could be used in mass-produced vehicles. Suzuki decided to take up the challenge and develop a rotary-engine motorcycle.

Many of the other Japanese motorcycle manufacturers had plans and/or prototypes for a rotary engine motorcycle, but it was Suzuki that went through a design and development program and actually manufactured and sold rotary motorcycles. The RE5 was very innovative, but like the Turbos to come in the 1980s, it was a technological dead-end. The RE5 promised to be the next leap forward after the GT750, but in the end, it almost ruined Suzuki. However, it

Riding an RE5

All RE5s are rather strange looking: the large lump of an engine with no cooling fins and no semblance in shape or size to any conventional piston engine; the very non-motorcyclelike carburetor with its interesting-looking intake manifold hanging off the left side, together with the exhaust system, with its finned crossover chamber and oval-shaped air intakes at the front of the pipes, this motorcycle lets you know that it is unconventional. The 1976 RE5 that I'm riding at least has conventional gauges and taillight—unlike the 1975, with its flip-top futuristic instrument panel and taillight canister.

I find starting the RE5 to be similar to the process of many other mid-1970s bikes, with a few exceptions. The first step in the process is to set the choke on the carburetor positioned on the left just behind the radiator. The next step is to turn the key on—but turning the key to its first position does not turn the ignition on. Instead, this position turns on three red warning lights (oil, oil pressure, and fuel) in the bottom of the tachometer. Turning the key to its next position powers up the ignition system, which produces a rather unnerving whistling that is loud enough to be mistaken for some kind of warning buzzer. After the ignition sound is dealt with, the rider presses the starter button and the engine starts with its characteristic sound.

While this routine is slightly different from the norm, the really interesting aspect of starting a rotary is the kick-starter. The RE5, like nearly all mid-1970s Japanese bikes, had a kick-starter lever. The problem with the RE5 kick-starter is that it is impossible to use it to start the engine. No, it's really more than that; due to the design of the kick-starter mechanism, you can't turn the engine over on an RE5 with the kick-starter.

After I press the starter button, the engine starts and the next thing that strikes me is the sound. The sound is a combination of whirring and chuffing and

(Continued on page 102)

(Continued from page 101)

when the engine is revved there is an additional whistling sound. The shift pattern on the bike is the standard down for first gear. Putting the bike in first and pulling away from a stop increases the volume and frequency of the sounds. As the bike accelerates the sounds coming from the engine all start to blend together. I accelerate and shift up through the gears and go down the entrance ramp to the highway. As I shift through the five-speed transmission, it seems conventional in nature, and the acceleration is comparable to a 750 of the RE5's era. An additional feature on the RE5 is the LED gear indicator, which always shows what gear you are in. The gear indicator is one of those features found on several Suzukis in the 1970s and early 1980s that I wish Suzuki had not stopped using. As we reach speed on the highway, I am impressed with the smoothness of the rotary engine. This bike is definitely suited for long-distance travel.

After going a few miles down the highway, I'm ready to try one of the sweeping exit ramps. As I go off the exit ramp, I am again impressed with the bike, as it is extremely stable going through the sweeping exit ramp turn. As I back off the throttle and slow down, I am again treated to another unusual sound. There is an interesting popping sound in the exhaust, definitely a characteristic sound for the rotary engine.

As I ride through slower traffic and finally reach my destination, several thoughts go through my mind. It's too bad that the RE5 wasn't more of a success for Suzuki. With more development, it could have turned out to be a great bike. As far as collectibility, the RE5 rates pretty high. It was very innovative when new, it was only available for two years and is therefore rather rare, and as far as looking different, there are not many motorcycles that look as unusual as the RE5. For riding, it's a great highway bike that you can cover some fairly long distance on in relative—remember, we are comparing this to other mid-1970s bikes—comfort. The bike is not my first pick for the real twisty back roads but for most riding it is very capable. All in all the RE5 is a very attractive bike to have in one's collection.

The RE5's engine was a single-rotor water-cooled Wankel engine displacing 497 cc. The engine was technologically very different from the typical motorcycle engine.

It was also very unusual looking and often referred to as having a lumplike appearance. There were not many things about the engine that appeared normal. Since the engine was water-cooled, there were no fins. Major engine components common to other motorcycle engines were located in unusual places or just looked weird. The oil filter was a typical—at least for cars—spin-on filter, but it was sticking out of the right side of the engine. The carburetor was nothing like most motorcycle carburetors. It had a strange appearance and was hanging off the left side of the engine.

On top of all of these unusual things the RE5 had three oil reservoirs. The engine oil was held in the engine sump and provided lubrication for the engine. The engine-injection oil was contained in a separate tank from which it was supplied to the carburetor float bowl to mix with the gasoline, much like a two-stroke engine. The third supply was the transmission oil.

Beyond the engine, the other parts of the RE5 were a mixture of the common, the unusual by necessity, and the just plain weird. The frame, suspension, and most of the other parts were standard Suzuki. There were dual disc brakes in the front and a drum in the rear. Telescopic front forks and a dual-shock rear swingarm. A nice dual seat and a reasonably common gas tank. All pretty standard stuff. The radiator and oil cooler were a little out of the norm, but the GT750 had already been out for a few years, so the radiator was not that unusual.

The exhaust was distinctly different. There was a single exhaust port on the front of the engine that went into a rather large finned chamber that fed into the two exhaust pipes. One pipe went back along each side of the bike with black heat shields on the mufflers. In addition to the strange, finned exhaust chamber at the front of the engine, there were also air intakes at the front of each exhaust pipe. The air intakes fed cool air into the double-walled exhaust pipes and were necessary, due to the high exhaust temperature of the rotary engine, to keep the exhaust pipe and muffler temperature down to a reasonable level. Beyond the strange looks of the exhaust were the instruments and the taillight. The speedometer, tachometer, water temperature gauge, and various warning lights were housed in the side of a strange-looking cylinder with reflectors on each end attached to the top of the headlight shell. This instrument cylinder had a flip-open plastic top. The taillight was also housed in a cylinder that mimicked the look of the instrument cylinder. This instrument and taillight configuration was only used on the 1975 RE5s with the 1976s getting the more common-looking instruments and taillight from the GT750.

The overall performance of the RE5 was also a mix. Straight-line performance was comparable to 750s of the day, but certainly nothing spectacular. The RE5 was slower through the quarter-mile than a GT750, but almost matched the GT750 for top speed. Through the turns, the RE5 was very stable with its long wheelbase. On the whole, handling was very good. The rotary engine was very smooth running, making for a virtually vibration-free ride. Fuel consumption, however, was quite high, so the cruising range was short.

In the end, the RE5 did not sell well. With its no better than average performance and its short cruising range, there was nothing particularly attractive about it. With its unusual engine and the related uncertainties of finding parts and maintenance, people weren't willing to take a chance with unproven (at least from a motorcyclist's point of view) engine technology. The RE5 was not widely accepted by motorcyclists and was not the success that Suzuki had hoped for. Fortunately for Suzuki, the GS family of four-cylinder, four-stroke engines was not too far in the distant future.

Today, the RE5 makes an interesting collectible. Because of the short two-year life of the bike, there are not many of them around. Concerns about the engine are much the same now as they were when the bikes were new. If there are problems with the engine, parts can be difficult to obtain, and finding a mechanic with experience with the engine is nearly impossible. On the other hand, the engines have proved to be very reliable and a good running RE5 with 50,000 miles on it is not unheard of. If you appreciate a bike with an unusual engine, different looks, and a unique sound, the RE5 is a perfect choice. The RE5 is such a unique motorcycle that care must be given to all aspects of it when considering one for purchase. The engine is obviously unique, as is the carburetor and exhaust system. While the 1976 model instruments and lighting are shared with the 1976 GT750, these parts are absolutely unique to the model and year on the 1975 RE5.

The 1976 RE5 had instruments and a taillight like the GT750 rather than the first year RE5's canisters. The shiny pipe just behind the radiator is the intake tube for the carburetor. Also note the small air scoops at the front of the exhaust pipes, which were used to help reduce the temperature of the exhaust system. *Author's collection*

The engine in the RE5 looked totally different than the conventional motorcycle engine. The bottom cylinder sticking out of the engine is the spin-on oil filter. *Suzuki Motor Corp., U.S.A.*

1977–1983, GS750 (748 cc)

Collectibility	★★★
Passenger Accommodations	★★★ 1/2
Reliability	★★★★
Parts/Service Availability	★★★★
Handling	★★★ 1/2
Engine Performance	★★★ 1/2

Engine	four cylinder, dual overhead cam, four-stroke
Bore & stroke	65x56.4 mm
Displacement	748 cc
Compression ratio	8.7:1
Bhp at rpm	60.17 at 8,500
Transmission	5 speed
Primary drive	straight cut gears
Clutch	multi disc, wet plate
Brakes: front	single disc
Brakes: rear	single disc
Tire size: front	3.25-19
Tire size: rear	4.00-18
Fuel capacity	4.95 gal
Wheelbase	58.7 in.
Weight	532 lb
Seat height	31.5 in.
Quarter-mile	12.75 sec at 104.77mph*
Top Speed	114 mph (estimated)

*Cycle magazine test, September 1976

The introduction of the GS750, together with the GS400, was a very significant event for Suzuki. The RE5 had just been taken off the market, the two-stroke triples were nearing the end of their life cycle, and Suzuki needed something to come back from the RE5 episode. It desperately needed a new successful motorcycle with a promising future. In 1977, Suzuki introduced the GS750, a motorcycle that would prove to be exactly what the company needed.

The GS750, while being significant as a very timely, successful new model, was also significant because it was an entirely new engine configuration for Suzuki. Prior to the GS750, all Suzukis, with the

The 1977 GS750 was one of the first of the very successful four-stroke Suzukis. The GS750 with spoke wheels and single disc brake was available for three years. *Suzuki Motor Corp., U.S.A.*

exception of the rotary engine RE5, had two-stroke engines with no more than three cylinders. The GS750 engine is a dual overhead cam, four-cylinder, four-stroke and was a complete departure from the previous formula. By choosing the four-cylinder, four-stroke engine configuration for the GS750, Suzuki was moving into a section of the market dominated by Honda and Kawasaki, and entered into direct competition with the well-established Honda CB750.

While the GS750 was a new design for Suzuki, there was nothing new or innovative about the bike when compared to the 750s being made by Honda and Kawasaki. The Suzuki engine had dual overhead cams with two valves per cylinder and a five-speed transmission. The exhaust system was a four-into-two with one muffler on each side of the bike and braking was by a single disc on the front and a single disc on the rear. The suspension was telescopic forks at the front and a twin-shock swingarm at the rear. All pretty standard fare. Two things, though, were noteworthy about the bike: it was Suzuki's first four-stroke and Suzuki got it right the first time. The GS750 was the success that Suzuki needed.

Over its model run the GS750 came in several states of trim:
* The base model, with spoke wheels and single front disc brake
* The E model, with cast wheels, dual front disc brakes, and a special dual seat
* The L model, with leading axle front forks, dual front disc brakes, pull back handlebars
* The T model, which was much like the L model

The GS750 was the first of Suzuki's four-stroke street bikes and a very important model for Suzuki. A dependable bike, available in many different versions, it makes an excellent choice for a person who likes to ride the bikes in his or her collection as well as look at them. With a little bit of searching a good GS750 should not be too hard to find. Look for a GS750 with good cosmetics and a sound exhaust system. As with all fours the GS750 exhaust is costly to replace.

The GS750L with pull-back handlebars, leading axle front forks, short exhaust, and stepped seat was the cruiser model of the GS750. This is the 1980 model. *Suzuki Motor Corp., U.S.A.*

1978–1983, GS1000 (997 cc)

The GS1000 was the large displacement version of the very successful Suzuki four-stroke GS series. This is a photo from a Suzuki ad for the 1978 GS1000E model with its cast wheels and dual front disc brakes. *Suzuki Motor Corp., U.S.A.*

Collectibility	★★★
Passenger Accommodations	★★★★
Reliability	★★★★
Parts/Service Availability	★★★★
Handling	★★★★
Engine Performance	★★★★

Engine	four cylinder, dual overhead cam, four-stroke
Bore & stroke	70.0x64.8 mm
Displacement	997 cc
Compression ratio	9.2:1
Bhp at rpm	74.52 at 8,000
Transmission	5 speed
Primary drive	helical gear
Clutch	multi disc, wet plate
Brakes: front	single disc
Brakes: rear	single disc
Tire size: front	3.25V19
Tire size: rear	4.00V18
Fuel capacity	4.8 gal
Wheelbase	58.66 in.
Weight	548 lb
Seat height	30.5 in.
Quarter-mile	11.89 sec at 113.35 mph*
Top Speed	135.14 mph*

Cycle magazine test, March 1978

The GS1000 was Suzuki's entry into the Superbike wars of the late 1970s. By 1978, Yamaha had introduced the XS11, Kawasaki the Z1R, and Honda had previewed the upcoming CBX. All of these bikes were fast and certainly Superbikes, but with the GS1000 Suzuki set a new standard as to what it would take in the future to be classified as a Superbike.

Although the GS1000 had a superb engine, there was a lot of emphasis placed on the handling capabilities of the machine. The basic suspension layout was the common telescopic forks at the front and a two-sided swingarm with twin shocks at the rear. What made it special was that the front forks had fittings to add or remove air to fine-tune the spring rate. A hand pump and an air gauge came with the bike, allowing the owner to adjust the air pressure in the forks to adjust the firmness of the forks or to compensate for the added weight of a fairing. At the rear, the shocks were adjustable for rebound dampening. A small adjuster on the top of the shocks allowed the shocks to be adjusted to four different settings. The GS1000 was the first production motorcycle with these types of suspension adjustments. This adjustable suspension, together with a very rigid frame, gave the GS1000 handling that was considered outstanding compared with the other Superbikes of the time.

The other aspect that Suzuki attacked was weight. The GS1000's competitors all were approaching the 600-pound mark, but the GS1000, with a full tank of gas, weighed just 548 pounds. The engine was 10 pounds lighter than the GS750 engine and the curb weight of the GS1000 was only 16 pounds more than the curb weight of the GS750.

The GS1000 engine was the standard transverse four-cylinder, four-stroke, with dual overhead cams and two valves per cylinder. There was the evolutionary change of the elimination of the kick-starter assembly, but nothing revolutionary. Perhaps the most important aspect of the GS1000 engine was its dependability. Many GS1000 engines were used for drag racing due to their high level of reliability.

Like the GS750, the GS1000 was available in several states of trim, including the base model, the E model, the L model, and the S model (more about the S models later). The GS1000 was also available as the GS1000G shaft-drive model.

So with the GS1000, Suzuki upped the requirements for what it took to qualify as a Superbike. Straight-line performance was not enough; handling improvements and weight reduction were now considerations. GS1000s are reasonably easy to find and for the collector of 1970s Superbikes, a GS1000 is quite an attractive piece with excellent performance and proven dependability. When buying a GS1000 look for good cosmetics but take care to ensure the engine is in good condition. While these engines are very dependable and can withstand a lot of abuse because of their very nature many of these bikes were driven very hard.

The GS1000 styling went through several changes over the production run. This is a 1980 GS1000E with a square headlight and leading axle forks. *Suzuki Motor Corp., U.S.A.*

The GS1000 was flexible and filled several roles for Suzuki. This is a 1980 GS1000GL with shaft drive and cruiser styling. In 1980 there was also the standard styled shaft drive GS1000G and the larger cruiser styled GS1100L. *Suzuki Motor Corp., U.S.A.*

This is a 1979 GS1000 with its spoked wheels and single front disc brakes. Very much like the 1978 model except for the paint scheme. *Suzuki Motor Corp., U.S.A.*

1979–1983, GS850 (843 cc)

Collectibility	★★ 1/2
Passenger Accommodations	★★★★
Reliability	★★★★
Parts/Service Availability	★★★★
Handling	★★★
Engine Performance	★★★

Engine	four cylinder, dual overhead cam, four-stroke
Bore & stroke	69x56.4 mm
Displacement	843 cc
Compression ratio	8.8:1
Bhp at rpm	n/a
Transmission	5 speed, shaft final drive
Primary drive	helical gear
Clutch	multi disc, wet plate
Brakes: front	dual disc
Brakes: rear	single disc
Tire size: front	3.50H19
Tire size: rear	4.50H17
Fuel capacity	5.8 gal
Wheelbase	59.1 in.
Weight	605 lb
Seat height	31.7 in.
Quarter-mile	12.97 sec at 104.77 mph*
Top Speed	n/a

Cycle magazine test, February 1979

The GS850, as the shaft drive model between the GS750 and the GS1000, was a great high-speed tourer. Not quite sporty enough to be classified as a sport tourer, it was nonetheless a marvelous motorcycle. This is the 1979 version. *Suzuki Motor Corp., U.S.A.*

In the mid-1970s, the Japanese motorcycle manufacturers recognized that there was an unfilled niche in the market for a shaft-drive motorcycle. BMW had been making shaft-drive motorcycles for years, but BMWs were expensive and didn't offer what everyone who wanted a shaft-drive motorcycle was looking for. Honda had been selling the Gold Wing since 1975, but the Gold Wing also did not suit all potential shaft-drive buyers. To satisfy this segment of the market, Yamaha had brought out the XS750 in 1976 and Honda had brought out the CX500 in 1978. Suzuki responded to the competition in 1979 with the introduction of the GS850.

The GS850 was based on both the GS750 and the GS1000. The cam and helical gear primary drive were from the GS1000, while the clutch and transmission were from the GS750, modified to accommodate the GS850's shaft drive. The engine was based on the GS750, bored out to yield a 95 cc displacement increase. The increased displacement helped offset the difference in weight between the 750 and the 850, but the straight-line performance of the GS850 was still not as good as the GS750. Quarter-mile time, as tested by Cycle magazine, was almost a quarter of a second slower for the GS850 than the GS750, but the terminal speed for both bikes was stated to be 104.77 miles per hour. (Interesting that the terminal speed was exactly the same.)

The GS850 suspension components were fairly standard for the time, with some additional features based on the GS1000. Front suspension was by telescopic fork with the addition of the air adjustment feature from the GS1000. Rear suspension was by twin-shock swingarm with the addition of rebound adjustment on the shocks, the same as the GS1000. The suspension setup gave the GS850 reasonable handling, and, together with the comfortable seat, gave the bike a nice ride.

The outcome of this mix of parts was a heavy but very competent motorcycle. The GS850 weighed 605 pounds with a full tank of gas, which was more than either the GS750 or the GS1000. The GS850 though was not about straight-line performance or handling. It was intended for people who wanted a well-executed shaft-drive motorcycle that was capable of covering distance quickly and comfortably and was an absolute pleasure to ride. The GS850 initially came in only one version equipped with cast wheels, a large gas tank, a very nice seat, fuel gauge, and gear indicator—plus, of course, the shaft drive. In 1980, the L model, with leading axle forks, pull back handlebars, and stepped seat was added. The GS850 package added up to a very complete motorcycle. Currently, GS850s come up for sale reasonably often and should not be difficult to find for someone looking for one. The GS850 is a very dependable motorcycle, but the shaft drive and all of the cosmetic items (tank, side cover, fenders, etc.) should be thoroughly checked on any GS850 you consider buying.

The GS1000S with its quarter fairing, low handlebars, and good-looking paint job was a very attractive bike and today is quite collectible. This is a 1980 model. *Suzuki Motor Corp., U.S.A.*

1979–1980, GS1000S (997 cc)

Collectibility	★★★ 1/2
Passenger Accommodations	★★★ 1/2
Reliability	★★★★
Parts/Service Availability	★★★★
Handling	★★★★
Engine Performance	★★★★

The GS1000S was primarily a restyled standard GS1000—or, if you like, a GS1000 café racer built by Suzuki. The GS1000S had an interesting quarter fairing (the fairing had a lower lip that Suzuki

A section of the Suzuki sales brochure for the GS1000S showing the quarter fairing and the fairing chin spoiler. *Suzuki Motor Corp., U.S.A.*

claimed increased down force on the front end at speed). It also featured low, narrow handlebars and an interesting paint job. Inside the quarter fairing was a clock, an oil temperature gauge, and a fuel gauge. Other than these additions, the bike was a GS1000. A significant point was that the GS1000S's styling was a definite step in the evolution of the pure sport bike.

Today, the GS1000S is an appealing motorcycle. Being based on the GS1000, it is a fast, good-handling, reliable motorcycle. With the fairing, low handlebars, and paint, you have an enticing factory-built café racer. Add to that the fact that the GS1000S was only available for two years and in small numbers, and you have a desirable motorcycle that is relatively rare and a bit more collectible than the other GS1000 models. If buying a GS1000S, be sure that the fairing is in good condition since these can be difficult to replace.

1982, GS1000SZ Katana (998 cc)

Collectibility	★★★★
Passenger Accommodations	★ 1/2
Reliability	★★★★
Parts/Service Availability	★★★★
Handling	★★★★
Engine Performance	★★★★

Engine	four cylinder, four valve/cylinder, dual overhead cam, four-stroke
Bore & stroke	69.4x66 mm
Displacement	998 cc
Compression ratio	9.5:1
Bhp at rpm	n/a
Transmission	5 speed
Primary drive	helical gear
Clutch	multi disc, wet plate
Brakes: front	dual disc
Brakes: rear	single disc
Tire size: front	3.50V19
Tire size: rear	4.50V17
Fuel capacity	5.8 gal
Wheelbase	59.8 in.
Weight	561 lb
Seat height	30.5 in.
Quarter-mile	11.256 sec at 120.64 mph*
Top Speed	141 mph*

* *Motorcyclist* magazine test, September 1981

Katana Nomenclature

A word about Katana nomenclature: The official designation for the first Katana was GS1000SZ Katana, with the Z indicating the 1982 model year. It would appear that this bike would also be called a GS1000S for short, but it is not. The name Katana is used when referring to this group of bikes or their more complete name Katana 1000 or Katana 1100 for the 1983 model. The GS1000S name is used only for the earlier model GS1000S.

The Katana was a GS1100 with a totally different look. While the Katana was a very capable motorcycle with an excellent engine, its looks were what made it such a significant motorcycle. To get this look, Suzuki went to Target Design in Germany. What Target Design gave Suzuki was the most radically designed production motorcycle to appear up to that time. With its quarter fairing, small windscreen, clip-on handlebars, stepped two-color seat, and dramatic lines, the Katana was a stunning motorcycle. Not everyone liked the look, but there was no denying that it was attention-grabbing and it could not be ignored on the street.

The Katana, with its dramatic lines, made an impact on motorcycle styling that had an effect for many years. This is the original 1982 GS1000S Katana. *Suzuki Motor Corp., U.S.A.*

Beyond the Katana's looks were its engine, suspension, and ride. The engine was based on the four valve per cylinder GS1100 engine, but with a smaller bore to bring the engine displacement down to under 1,000 cc. The reduced displacement allowed the bike to qualify for AMA Superbike racing. While not the quickest bike on the street, the Katana still performed at a level very close to the GS1100's with only slightly lower quarter-mile times.

The Katana's suspension was different than Suzuki's other large displacement street bikes. The early Katana's suspension was very stiff, with every bump and ripple in the pavement transmitted to the rider. While the stiff suspension worked well at high speed on smooth pavement, it was too stiff for most street riding. The stiff suspension, coupled with the riding position required by the stepped seat, clip-ons, and footpeg position made the Katana uncomfortable for long-distance riding.

But ride comfort was not what the Katana was intended for. It was intended to have liter bike performance in a factory-built café racer that had eye-catching looks. The Katana succeeded very well at what it was intended to do. It also influenced the design of many motorcycles that followed it and led to the long line of Suzuki motorcycles that today still use the Katana name and follow the spirit of the first Katana.

In 1983 the Katana engine was enlarged to 1100 cc and improvements were made to the suspension. The Katana retained its unique styling, though, with only subtle changes distinguishing the Katana 1100 from the Katana 1000. *Suzuki Motor Corp., U.S.A.*

In 1983, some changes were made that gave us the GS1100SD Katana. The engine was enlarged to 1,100 cc, due to changes in AMA Superbike rules that restricted the Superbike class to 750 cc. The increased displacement gave the Katana a boost in performance, making it the fastest production motorcycle in the quarter-mile in 1983. Changes were also made to soften up the suspension to give the bike a better ride and to improve the handling. The changes made for a faster, better handling, more comfortable motorcycle. Fortunately, designers retained the radical styling of the previous year's Katana. In 1983, this styling was also used on the smaller GS750SD Katana.

As with other bikes that had a short production run, the first and second year Katanas are hard to find. When you do find one, be sure that all the bodywork and the seat are present and in good condition. If not, be sure to adjust the price accordingly but bear in mind that these items will be very difficult to find. When looking for a Katana, go for the 1982 if you prefer the first-year model with its lack of compromise, or go for the 1983 if you prefer better performance and ride. More than likely it will be best to buy whichever year you find first so that you'll have a Katana to ride while you look for the one you want.

1983, XN85 Turbo (673 cc)

Collectibility	★★★★
Passenger Accommodations	★★★
Reliability	★★★
Parts/Service Availability	★★★
Handling	★★★★
Engine Performance	★★★★ 1/2

Engine	four cylinder, dual overhead cam, four-stroke, turbo-charged
Bore & stroke	62x55.8 mm
Displacement	673 cc
Compression ratio	7.4:1
Bhp at rpm	71.43 at 6,500
Transmission	5 speed
Primary drive	helical gear
Clutch	multi disc, wet plate
Brakes: front	dual disc
Brakes: rear	single disc
Tire size: front	100/90H16
Tire size: rear	120/90H17
Fuel capacity	5.0 gal
Wheelbase	58.7 in.
Weight	552.5 lb
Seat height	30.5 in.
Quarter-mile	11.99 sec at 110.02 mph*
Top Speed	133 mph*

*Cycle magazine test, December 1982

The XN85 was Suzuki's entry into the Turbo bike contest of the mid-1980s. Suzuki thought, as did Honda, Kawasaki, Yamaha, and many of the automotive manufacturers, that turbocharging was the technology of the future for high-performance vehicles. Turbocharging

The XN85 was Suzuki's turbocharged motorcycle and was only available in 1983. The XN85 was not only fast but also had a sophisticated suspension and handled very well. *Turbo Motorcycle International Owners Association*

was promoted to the public as a method to get more power out of an engine essentially for free. Suzuki, like the other manufacturers, however, quickly realized that the negative aspects of turbocharging outweighed the positive aspects and that the public was not interested in dealing with its problems to get the performance increase. Like most of the turbo bikes, the XN85 was very interesting but very short-lived. The Suzuki Turbo was, in fact, only available in 1983.

The XN85, like the Yamaha Seca Turbo and the Honda CX650 Turbo, was based on a 650 cc engine. The engine was a four-cylinder, dual overhead cam with two valves per cylinder. Fuel delivery was by electronic fuel injection, which Honda and Kawasaki also used on their turbos, and unlike Yamaha's carbureted fuel system. The compression ratio, typical for a turbocharged motor, was a rather low 7.4:1. Power for the Suzuki engine was rated at 71.43 horsepower at 8,000 rpm. The quarter-mile time just broke the 12-second mark at 11.99 seconds—a solid half-second faster than the Yamaha Seca Turbo and almost four-tenths of a second faster than the Honda CX500 Turbo.

To a Suzuki enthusiast, one of the interesting features of the XN85 was the use of the Ram Air System that was similar to the earlier two-strokes, such as the GT380 and GT500. In the XN85, though, the Ram Air was fed by cooling ducts in the bike's fairing.

The XN85 styling, while not as radical as the Katana, was solidly based on the Katana styling of the previous year. The small half-fairing, stepped seat, and general lines were all Katana-inspired. As with the Katana, you either liked it or you didn't; there was not much in between.

The XN85's handling was considered excellent and suspension advances were as significant as the turbocharged engine. The front forks had a two-position adjustment for spring preload. The front tire was a 100/90H16, giving the XN85 very quick steering response. It was the first application of a 16-inch tire on a production street bike. The rear suspension featured Suzuki's Full Floater shock system, its version of the single shock rear end, and a box-section swingarm. The rear suspension was also adjustable for preload.

Being a turbocharged motorcycle, the XN85 is automatically a desirable collectible, and since it was only on the market for one year, it is very rare as well. As with all of the turbo bikes, if you decide that you must have one for your collection, make sure that the turbocharger is in good working order. Not all owners took proper care of their turbos and replacing it can be an expensive proposition. Also, since it was a single year model, a buyer should be sure that all of the bodywork and other parts unique to the bike are present and in good condition as these parts are difficult to locate.

Future collectibles
1986–Present, GSX-R750 (749 cc)

Collectibility	★★
Passenger Accommodations	★★
Reliability	★★★★
Parts/Service Availability	★★★★
Handling	★★★★★
Engine Performance	★★★★ 1/2

Engine	four cylinder, four valve/cylinder, dual overhead cam, four-stroke, air and oil cooled
Bore & stroke	70x48.7 mm
Displacement	749 cc
Compression ratio	10.6:1
Bhp at rpm	79.26 at 10,500
Transmission	6 speed
Primary drive	straight cut gear
Clutch	multi disc, wet plate
Brakes: front	dual disc with dual piston calipers
Brakes: rear	single disc with dual piston caliper
Tire size: front	110/80VR18
Tire size: rear	140/70VR18
Fuel capacity	5.5 gal
Wheelbase	57.3 in.
Weight	465.5 lb
Seat height	30.6 in.
Quarter-mile	11.33 sec at 114.79 mph*
Top Speed	146 mph*

*Cycle magazine test, February 1986

When introduced to the U.S. market in 1986, the GSX-R750 exhibited a level of performance seldom seen on a street-going 750. The GSX-R750 was a street bike that was only a touch away from being an out-and-out race bike. Like the Yamaha FZ750, the GSX-R750 sharpened the distinction between sport bikes and other motorcycles.

The 1986 GSX-R750 was a definite indicator of the future trend in sport bikes. With its light weight and spectacular performance, the GSX-R750 was one of the top sport bikes from the mid-1980s through the 1990s. *Suzuki Motor Corp., U.S.A.*

The GSX-R750 in many ways exemplified further development and refinement of the technology that Suzuki had been using in its previous sport bikes. The engine was a four valve per cylinder, four-cylinder four-stroke. The engine was cooled innovatively by a combination of air and oil cooling. Power output was rated at just over 79 horsepower at 10,500 rpm. Straight-line performance was almost identical to the FZ750, with a quarter-mile time of 11.33 seconds.

The most innovative feature of the GSX-R750 was its light weight. When the bike was designed, engineers saved weight everywhere possible. Aluminum was used for many components, including the frame, footpegs, shift lever, brake lever, shock linkages, and swingarm and other suspension components. The weight of the crankshaft, the head, the connecting rods, and the engine case were reduced to lighten the engine. Even fasteners had hollowed-out heads to save weight. The result of this weight-saving program was that the curb weight of the bike with a full tank of gas was just over 465 pounds. This made the GSX-R750 almost 60 pounds lighter than the FZ750.

The handling of the GSX-R750 was also distinctive. During the 1980s, tires had continued to get larger and Suzuki's suspension design continued to be more refined. These continuing developments, coupled with the GSX-R's light weight, produced a bike with cutting-edge handling.

Since the bike's introduction, Suzuki has continued to develop it. For more than 10 years, the GSX-R750 has been Suzuki's 750 cc-class sport bike. As it was when it was introduced, the Suzuki continues to be a prominent force in the class. With the switch to liquid cooling in the later GSX-R750s, I think it's a safe bet that the early air/oil cooled GSX-R750s will be future collectibles. Eventually, perhaps even the entire model line will qualify. While the GSX-R750 is a newer motorcycle than many in this book and parts are more readily available, it is still a very sophisticated motorcycle. Care should be given to all aspects of any motorcycle that you look to buy to be sure that there are no missing or damaged parts that will require replacement. Attention to these details will save much aggravation and many dollars if you want your GSX-R750 to be at its best.

Chapter 4

Yamaha

MODELS COVERED

YDS2	R5	XS1100
YG-1	XS1	XV750H Virago
YJ2	TX750	XJ650LJ Seca Turbo
YM1	RD350	V-Max
YL1	XS750	FZ750

Yamaha was founded in 1897 by Torakusu Yamaha as the Nippon Gakki Co. Yamaha had begun building organs in 1887, and the primary business of his new company was the manufacture of musical instruments. The company prospered and became one of the premier musical instrument manufacturers in the world. This is the basis for Yamaha's logo with three crossed tuning forks.

In Yamaha's early ads, not only did the company try to sell motorcycles but it also tried to sell itself, tell you who the U.S. distributor was, where their eastern branch was located, and solicit new dealers. This ad, promoting the features of the 250 cc YD-S Sports, in addition to all of the other information, appeared in the July 1961 issue of *Motorcyclist* magazine. *Yamaha Motor Corporation, USA*

In 1950, Nippon Gakki named Genichi Kawakami its fourth president. Kawakami took on his new job with an interest in expanding and diversifying Nippon Gakki's business into new areas. He evaluated available company resources and prospective business opportunities, and after careful consideration, made the decision that the new business venture would be the design and manufacture of motorcycles.

In January of 1955, the first Yamaha motorcycle, the 125 cc YA-1, was built. A few short months later, in July of 1955, Yamaha Motor Co., Ltd. was founded. With the design of the YA-1 engine, Yamaha decided to the follow the same path as many of the other manufacturers of the time and based the two-stroke YA-1 engine on the highly successful DKW RT125 design. At the time, DKW was recognized as a leading designer of two-stroke engines, and several other noted manufacturers, including Harley Davidson and BSA, had successfully built two-stroke engines based on the DKW design. The 1955 introduction of the YA-1 also coincided with the first year for the running of the Asama Road Race at Mount Asama, north of Tokyo. Several YA-1s were entered in the Asama race and their dominance of the race provided great publicity for Yamaha.

The YA-1 proved to be so successful that Yamaha decided to introduce a new model that was once again heavily influenced by DKW—the 175 cc YC-1.

Shortly after the introduction of the YC-1 came Yamaha's third bike: the YD1, which proved to be very important to the future of the company. The decision was made that the new motorcycle would be a 250 and Yamaha management thought that the best approach to designing the new bike would be to base the design on yet another successful German design, the Adler MB250. But the designers at Yamaha had a different approach. They felt that they had learned enough from the YA-1 and the YC-1, and they wanted to design the new 250 based on their own concepts. It is a credit to Yamaha and its management that this is the approach that was taken. The YD-1 was the first all-Yamaha design and it proved to be very successful.

The next Asama Road Race was held in 1957 and once again, Yamaha was very successful, taking first and second place in the 125 cc class, and first, second, and third place in the 250 cc class. Yamaha was now ready to contest events outside of Japan, and in doing so, to take a major step toward entering the U.S. market.

In 1958, Yamaha entered the race on Catalina Island off the coast of Los Angeles. The race was an off road event, not particularly large or important, but it was Yamaha's first race outside of Japan. After a fall and a pit stop to change a spark plug, the Yamaha entry finished sixth. Not a spectacular finish, but one that Yamaha was pleased with. In hindsight, this sixth-place finish in a rather small event can be seen as Yamaha's first in a long line of successes in racing around the world.

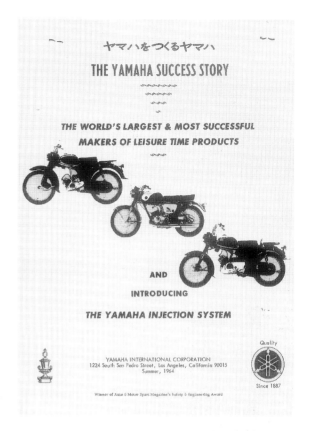

This is the cover of a brochure that Yamaha put together and sent out to Yamaha piano dealers in June of 1964 to acquaint them with the Motorcycle Division. The brochure gives some sales figures for the company, lists the different lines of Yamaha products, and then goes on for the next 12 pages highlighting the successes of the Motorcycle Division. Included are five pages of description, photos, and diagrams of the operation and advantages of the Yamaha Injection System. *Yamaha Motor Corporation, USA*

The Catalina race also marked the entrance of Yamaha into the American motorcycle market. In December of 1958 there was a short article in the back pages of Cycle magazine titled "The Yamaha From Tokyo." Accompanying the text were two small photos, one labeled "'Yamaha 125 cc" and the other "Yamaha 250 cc". The article, in order to educate the reader, starts with the phrase, "The YAMAHA (pronounced Yah-mah-ha)". The article goes on to highlight the Catalina race, Yamaha's history, and the company's position amongst the 30-plus motorcycle manufacturers in operation in Japan at that time. The article finishes by giving the address for the Yamaha factory branch office in Los Angeles. Such a small start for a company that has accomplished so much in the ensuing 40-plus years.

1963–1964, YDS2 (246 cc)

Collectibility	★★★★
Passenger Accommodations	★★ 1/2
Reliability	★★ 1/2
Parts/Service Availability	★★
Handling	★★ 1/2
Engine Performance	★★

Engine	vertical twin, piston port, two-stroke
Bore & stroke	2.21 in. x 1.97 in.
Displacement	246 cc
Compression ratio	8.0:1
Bhp at rpm	25 at 7,500
Transmission	5 speed
Primary drive	gear
Clutch	multi disc, wet plate
Brakes: front	twin-leading-shoe drum
Brakes: rear	single-leading-shoe drum
Tire size: front	2.75-18
Tire size: rear	3.00-18
Fuel capacity	4.1 gal
Wheelbase	50.8 in.
Weight	338 lb
Seat height	30.5 in.
Quarter-mile	16.9 sec at 75 mph*
Top Speed	90 mph*

*Cycle World magazine test, January 1963

The YDS2 was Yamaha's 250 cc road machine for 1963. It was the largest bike that the company made that year, and it was the flagship of the Yamaha lineup. Interestingly, the YDS2 was not only the largest Yamaha built in 1963, but with the exception of the Honda 305s, the YDS2 and the Suzuki 250 were the largest displacement motor-cycles being imported from the entire country of Japan.

The YDS2 engine was a twin-cylinder, piston-port, two-stroke with a 180-degree crankshaft. The Yamaha Autolube system had not been introduced yet, so lubrication was by gas/oil premix. Claimed horsepower for the YDS2 was 25 horsepower at 7,500 rpm and with the rather uncommon five-speed transmission, acceleration was brisk for an early 1960s 250. Performance in the *Cycle World* test of January 1963 showed a quarter-mile time of 16.0 seconds at 75 miles per hour with a top speed of 90 miles per hour.

The *Cycle World* test also scored the YDS2's overall performance quite favorably, with the exception of the suspension. During a quick lap at Riverside Raceway, the writer noted that the bike moved up and down on its suspension and was very difficult to hold on line. The test results further indicated that for daily riding, the suspension was adequate. And the writer concluded that with the level of performance of the rest of the bike, it was quite probable that most YDS2 buyers would eventually ride the bike hard enough to encounter the shortcomings in the suspension.

The YDS2 is interesting, since it represents the peak level of technology that Yamaha had attained in the early 1960s. On one hand, the displacement of the engine is quite small when compared to the Nortons and Harleys of the same period, but on the other, the level of performance generated by the engine is quite impressive. The YDS2 was certainly an indicator of the coming level of performance that Yamaha would reach with the two-stroke engine. For the enthusiast of early Yamahas, the YDS2, while hard to find, is a fascinating motorcycle worth pursuing. Any YSD2 being considered for purchase should be carefully checked for missing and nonoriginal parts, since all parts for a YDS2 are hard to find.

YAMAHA INTERNATIONAL CORPORATION
1224 SOUTH SAN PEDRO STREET • LOS ANGELES 15, CALIFORNIA
Telephone: 748-0237

SINCE 1887

June 5, 1964

TO OUR PIANO DEALERS:

Many of you people have expressed interest from time to time in the growth of our Motorcycle Division. As you probably are aware, the fantastic newfound popularity of the lightweight sports motorcycle has made it possible for our Motorcycle Division to enjoy phenomenal growth.

Recently, Mr. James E. Jingu, who is in charge of advertising and public relations for the Motorcycle Division, arranged preparation of the enclosed brochure which tells the story of the growth of this Division of our Company. Mr. Bert Smith, who is Sales Manager for the Motorcycle Division, has made available sufficient copies so that we could send each of our piano dealers one booklet.

You will find some confusion in the various statistics as to employees and sales volume. For example, the figure of 13,000 employees includes not only those employed by Yamaha Motors, but also Nippon Gakki, which is the parent company and manufacturers of pianos and musical instruments. The sales volume reported on page 1 for the Los Angeles based operation refers only to motorcycles and does not include figures for the Music Division. When such figures are added, sales approximated $11 million.

The Piano Division is currently reinvesting the majority of its profits in development plans for the future. Thus, our present earning capacity in the division is not as strong as it otherwise would be. This opportunity is made possible for us because of the remarkable growth of the Motorcycle Division. It would be sensible for us to remember, therefore, that the growth of our Piano Division is being enhanced by the profits from our partner, the Motorcycle Division.

We have congratulated Mr. Smith and Mr. Jingu and the members of their field organization for the excellence of their work for the fiscal year just completed.

Sincerely,

Everett S. Rowan
General Sales Manager

ESR/ms
Enclosure

Known the World Over —YAMAHA Pianos—YAMAHA Motorcycles

This letter was stapled into the cover of the brochure Yamaha sent to its piano dealers. It's interesting to read in the third paragraph about Yamaha reinvesting profits in the piano division and that "It would be sensible for us (the piano dealers) to remember therefore that the growth of our Piano Division is being enhanced by the profits from our partner, the Motorcycle Division." The years since then have proved that this arrangement was advantageous for both divisions. *Yamaha Motor Corporation, USA*

1964–1966, YG1 (73 cc)

Collectibility	★★
Passenger Accommodations	★
Reliability	★★
Parts/Service Availability	★★
Handling	★ 1/2
Engine Performance	★

A photo of a family of four sitting on new Yamahas in front of a dealer's shop shows the change that motorcycling was going through in the 1960s. The Japanese manufacturers made motorcycling a family activity and acceptable for everyone. In the window in the background can be seen sales banners for the YD-2, YG-1, and YDT-1. *Yamaha Motor Corporation, USA*

Engine	single cylinder, rotary valve, two-stroke
Bore & stroke	47x42 mm
Displacement	73 cc
Compression ratio	6.8:1
Bhp at rpm	6.6 at 7,000
Transmission	4 speed
Primary drive	gear
Clutch	multi disc, wet plate
Brakes: front	single-leading-shoe drum
Brakes: rear	single-leading-shoe drum
Tire size: front	2.50-17
Tire size: rear	2.50-17
Fuel capacity	1.7 gal
Wheelbase	45.1 in.
Weight	140 lb
Seat height	n/a
Quarter-mile	n/a
Top Speed	53 mph claimed

The YG1 was one of Yamaha's early successes. With its light weight and 80 cc two-stroke engine, it was easy enough for a newcomer to use and yet quick enough to be fun to ride. *Yamaha Motor Corporation, USA*

The YG-1 Rotary Jet was like many of the Japanese motorcycles that were imported into the United States during the 1960s. The engine was typical of Yamaha small displacement bikes of the era: a single-cylinder, rotary-valve two-stroke. The first YG-1 was sold before the introduction of Autolube, so engine lubrication was by the traditional fuel-oil premix, while the later YG-1 made use of the Autolube system. Since the engine was rotary-valve, the carburetor was located on the side of the engine and hidden under the engine side cover. The bike's performance was quite good for its engine size, with a top speed of a little under 55 miles per hour.

A large part of what makes the YG-1 an interesting motorcycle, in addition to its mechanical features, was its appearance and styling, which brought together many of the styling characteristics found on other early 1960s Japanese motorcycles. The chain on the YG-1 was fully enclosed, which was very functional, keeping the chain lubricated and extending its life. The front fender of the YG-1 wrapped around the sides of the tire, and there was a mudflap on the back edge of the front fender. In the same vein there was also a small flap that extended off the back fender. These fender details were all functional in nature and were intended to keep the rider dry in wet weather. From a styling point of view, though, enclosed chain guards and fender flaps were not stylish and were used less and less over the next few years. Another item was the YG-1's speedometer, which resided in a nacelle in the top of the headlight assembly. This also went out of style in the late 1960s when the headlight and the gauges became separate assemblies. To complete the styling, the YG1 had turn signals. Many of the first Japanese motorcycles that were imported into the United States had turn signals, which eventually disappeared on succeeding models only to reappear in the late 1960s. I'm sure, though, that the reintroduction of turn signals had more to do with the laws of the time than it did with styling.

The YG-1 is an interesting example of an early 1960s Yamaha. While these are not as common as many motorcycles, they should definitely be considered by any collector of early Yamaha motorcycles. Since it is uncommon, any YG1 you consider for your collection needs to be checked carefully for missing and nonoriginal parts.

1965–1966, YJ2 Riverside 60 (60 cc)

Collectibility	★★ 1/2
Passenger Accommodations	★
Reliability	★★
Parts/Service Availability	★★
Handling	★ 1/2
Engine Performance	★

Engine	single cylinder, two-stroke, rotary valve
Bore & stroke	42x42 mm
Displacement	60 cc
Compression ratio	7.1:1
Bhp at rpm	5.0 at 7,000
Transmission	4 speed
Primary drive	helical gear
Clutch	multi disc, wet plate
Brakes: front	single-leading-shoe drum
Brakes: rear	single-leading-shoe drum
Tire size: front	2.25-17
Tire size: rear	2.25-17
Fuel capacity	1.33 gal
Wheelbase	45.8 in.
Weight	161 lb
Seat height	n/a
Quarter-mile	n/a
Top Speed	50–55 mph claimed

An interesting mix of styling can be seen in this YJ2. The flared front fender, flap on the rear fender, heel and toe shifter, and enclosed chain guard were going out of style by the mid-1960s. The chrome-sided gas tanks would be around for a few more years but would also soon disappear. The high-level street scrambler exhaust, however, would remain popular into the mid-1970s. Power was provided by a rotary valve 60 cc single. This is a YJ2 Riverside 60. *Yamaha Motor Corporation, USA*

The YJ1 was closely related to the YJ2, both in engine and in styling. This photo of a 1965 YJ1 was taken in the late spring of 1966. Since the bike ran premix and Roger says he always erred on the side of safety, a blue haze always followed them as they explored the back roads and dirt paths around Pensacola, Florida. *Roger Cole*

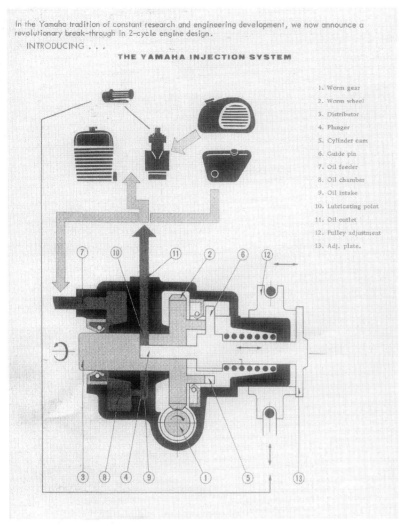

In the Yamaha tradition of constant research and engineering development, we now announce a revolutionary break-through in 2-cycle engine design.

INTRODUCING . . .

THE YAMAHA INJECTION SYSTEM

1. Worm gear
2. Worm wheel
3. Distributor
4. Plunger
5. Cylinder cam
6. Guide pin
7. Oil feeder
8. Oil chamber
9. Oil intake
10. Lubricating point
11. Oil outlet
12. Pulley adjustment
13. Adj. plate.

The Yamaha Injection System made dealing with the lubrication needed by a two-stroke motorcycle much easier. As Yamaha stated, it was a "revolutionary break-through in 2-cycle engine design." *Yamaha Motor Corporation, USA*

The YJ2, also known as the Riverside 60, was one of Yamaha's mid-1960s small displacement bikes. The engine was a 60 cc two-stroke, rotary-valve single. The Autolube oil-injection system was part of the specification, so premixing of gas and oil was unnecessary. Top speed for the Yamaha YJ2 was claimed to be 50–55 miles per hour and fuel consumption was claimed to be a very frugal 200 miles per gallon. Accommodations for the rider were adequate, but riding two up was quite a challenge, particularly if either person was of greater than average size.

Styling of the YJ2 was in some ways a holdover from an earlier time and yet in other ways, it was very up to date. The front fender was deep and covered a large portion of the front tire. A throwback to the previous decade's styling, the back of the fender was flared out. In addition, the J1 sported a fully enclosed chain guard, which although functional, was not very stylish. On the more up-to-date end of the styling spectrum, there was a dual seat and high-level street scrambler–style exhaust. As an added touch, there was the little rubber mud flap sticking straight out from the rear fender, very similar to the Honda Super Hawks.

For those with an interest in small displacement motorcycles, the YJ2 is an attractive bike. The look of the bike, with the mix of old and new styling is a good example of the changes that were taking place in motorcycle styling in the mid-1960s. The chrome tank panels, rubber knee grips on the tank, and overall styling are very attractive if you are looking for something from this era. The Yamaha two-stroke engine gave a performance edge over bikes of the time like the Honda Sport 50, and with the Autolube system, the messy process of premixing the gas and oil was eliminated. The main thing is the fact that YJ2s are now rarely seen and are not nearly as common as something like a Honda S65. Of course, this uniqueness may make for a long search if you want a YJ2. Parts for YJ2s are very hard to find, and a YJ2 should be thoroughly checked for completeness and originality since any items that need to be replaced will require a lot of searching.

1965–1966, YM-1 (305 cc)

Collectibility	★★★ 1/2
Passenger Accommodations	★★
Reliability	★★ 1/2
Parts/Service Availability	★★
Handling	★★ 1/2
Engine Performance	★★ 1/2

Engine	twin cylinder, two-stroke
Bore & stroke	60x54 mm
Displacement	305 cc
Compression ratio	7.1:1
Bhp at rpm	29 at 7,000
Transmission	5 speed
Primary drive	helical gear
Clutch	multi disc, wet plate
Brakes: front	twin-leading shoe drum
Brakes: rear	single-leading shoe drum
Tire size: front	3.00-18
Tire size: rear	3.00-18
Fuel capacity	4.7 gal
Wheelbase	51.0 in.
Weight	343 lb
Seat height	30.8 in.
Quarter-mile	15.1 sec at 83 mph*
Top Speed	98 mph*

Cycle World magazine test, July 1966

The 305 cc YM-1 was also known as the "Cross Country." The current owner of this 1966 YM-1 was fortunate to obtain the bike from the estate of the original owner. Very little was required to bring it to the state shown in this picture. *Rick Seto*

As most Yamahas were by 1966, the YM-1 was equipped with the Autolube system, making gas and oil premixing, and all the associated problems, obsolete. This bike proudly displays not only an Autolube sticker but also a Yamaha injection system sticker on its side cover. With the Autolube system all the owner had to do was check the sight glass, seen next to the Autolube sticker, to be sure there was enough two-stroke oil in the oil tank. *Rick Seto*

The YM-1, although carrying a different nomenclature, was the next step in the development of the YDS series. The engine was developed from the YDS3 and included improvements such as a stronger crankshaft and redesigned connecting rods. In addition to the design detail changes, the YM-1 enjoyed a displacement increase over the YDS3 to 305 cc. The compression ratio, however, was slightly lower in the YM-1, so the displacement increase only yielded a 20-percent power increase. The result of this was that the YM-1, with increased torque and power, was an easier bike to ride. Pulling away from a stop required less finessing of the throttle and clutch than the YDS3 did. In addition, the YM-1 engine was very smooth all the way up to 7,000 rpm. This meant that for most day-to-day use and for cruising on the highway at speeds as high as 70 miles per hour, there was almost no vibration.

The Autolube system, famous by this time, provided the lubrication for the engine. No more mixing of gas and oil for this two-stroke. All the rider had to do was make sure that the oil tank

Yamaha Autolube

One of the problems with a two-stroke engine has been the need for the oil to be mixed with the gasoline in order to lubricate the engine. Up until the mid-1960s, this was done by mixing the oil with the gasoline by hand when filling the gas tank. If the rider bought 3.1 gallons of gasoline, he needed to calculate the amount of oil to add to the gas tank to get a 20:1 gasoline-to-oil ratio.

After punching the buttons on my calculator (you'll recall that these were not in existence in the 1960s), I know that 0.155 gallons of oil is needed to get the 20:1 ratio for 3.1 gallons of gasoline. After doing the mental calculations, the rider knew that he needed to add a little over half a quart of oil (he also had to calculate that 0.155 gallons is 0.62 quarts) to the gas tank to get the correct mixture. The rider added somewhere between half and three-quarters of a quart and ended up with a ratio of between 16.5:1 and 24.8:1. Not very precise even if you could do the math.

With the Autolube system, introduced in 1964, Yamaha eliminated these problems. Autolube consisted of a variable displacement pump, an oil tank, and the necessary plumbing to inject oil directly into the intake port. The engine drove the pump and its output increased as the engine speed increased. The pump's piston stroke was variable and was controlled by a cable connected to the throttle, so the output of the pump was also dependent on the load on the engine. With this setup, the fuel/oil ratio varied from 20:1 at full throttle to about 200:1 when the throttle was closed and the engine was at idle. This system eliminated the calculations for the amount of oil needed and the inaccuracies of measuring the oil. Autolube also reduced the number of fouled spark plugs and the smoky trail left by a two-stroke running on premix. The fault with the system was that the pump was driven from the transmission and was thus disconnected from its drive source when the clutch was disengaged. Because of this it was not considered to be a good idea to sit at a traffic light with the clutch pulled in, revving the motor. In actuality, the system worked well even with this apparent design inadequacy.

never ran dry. This was certainly a step forward from the problems associated with premixing the gas and oil.

The YM-1's handling was considered very good at the time, with no readily perceptible nasty habits. It was possible, however, as with many bikes of the time, to touch parts of the underside on the pavement when the bike was pushed to the extreme. Steering damping was by means of a knob that was tightened or loosened to dial in the appropriate amount of friction to eliminate any front-end wobble.

One of the interesting idiosyncrasies of the YM-1 was its tachometer. The tachometer was driven off the transmission mainshaft and thus received no drive when the clutch was disengaged. Rev the engine with the bike in neutral and the clutch engaged and the tachometer indicated the engine speed, but pull the clutch lever and the tachometer dropped to zero. This made for a rather interesting situation if you had any desire to see how fast the engine was turning over before you let out the clutch. It's also interesting to note that the tachometer drive setup was like the Autolube system in that it, too, ceased to work when the clutch was disengaged.

The YM-1 is an attractive bike since it was very similar to the YDS3 but had a larger engine with better performance characteristics. While just about as seldom seen as the YDS3, the YM-1 is attractive since it represents another of the steps in the development of Yamaha's line of performance-oriented two-stroke street motorcycles. YM-1s are easier to find parts for than the models covered so far in this chapter—although be sure the gas tank and exhaust are in good condition, as these can be difficult to replace.

The YM-1 right side showing the Autolube oil tank and the twin-leading-shoe front drum brake setup. *Rick Seto*

1966–1967, YL1 (98 cc)

Collectibility	★★★
Passenger Accommodations	★ 1/2
Reliability	★★ 1/2
Parts/Service Availability	★★
Handling	★ 1/2
Engine Performance	★ 1/2

The 1966 YL1, the kick-start version of the Twin Jet 100. The YL1 and the electric start YL1E differed very little in appearance. *Hal Toomer*

Engine	twin cylinder, piston port, two-stroke
Bore & stroke	38x43 mm
Displacement	98 cc
Compression ratio	7.1:1
Bhp at rpm	9.5 at 8,500 claimed
Transmission	4 speed
Primary drive	helical gear
Clutch	multi-disc, wet plate
Brakes: front	single-leading-shoe drum
Brakes: rear	single-leading-shoe drum
Tire size: front	2.50-17
Tire size: rear	2.50-17
Fuel capacity	1.95 gal
Wheelbase	45.1 in.
Weight	180 lb
Seat height	n/a
Quarter-mile	n/a
Top Speed	60 mph*

Cycle World magazine "Road Impression," March 1966

This is the YL1E version of the Twin Jet 100. The E in the nomenclature indicates that this is an electric-start model. This bike has the Yamaha luggage rack and small chrome turn signals. Although the turn signals were not commonly found on YL1s, or most of the other Japanese bikes sold in 1967, they were sometimes added by the owner. Also some bikes sold in Canada had turn signals and this bike may have originally been sold in Canada. *Perry Ritter*

The YL1, commonly referred to as the Twin Jet 100, was introduced in 1966. The name Twin Jet reflected the engine configuration: a twin-cylinder, piston-port two-stroke. This engine represented a departure from common Yamaha practice of the time for small displacement models, in that up to the YL1, the sub-100 cc Yamahas were rotary-valve singles. Common opinion was that a rotary-valve engine was superior to a piston-port engine for making power, yet here Yamaha had introduced a new model in a popular displacement class with a piston-port engine.

Yamaha wanted to make sure that the public appreciated the virtues of its new model, so the Twin Jet sales brochures raved about the engine's performance and how "with twin cylinders, and twin carburetors, you get four times the smoothness of a single 4-stroke." It is interesting to note that the model introduced after the YL1 was the YL2 Rotary Jet. The YL2 was a rotary-valve single, a return to earlier Yamaha practice.

The YL1 was popular when introduced and remains popular today. While not as common as later, larger displacement Yamahas, YL1s do come up for sale from time to time and should be added to the collection of anyone interested in early small displacement Yamahas. When buying a YL1, all cosmetic parts (gas tank, exhaust, seat, etc.) should be checked carefully to be sure they are in good condition and do not require replacement.

1970–1972, R5 (347 cc)

Collectibility	★★★ 1/2
Passenger Accommodations	★★ 1/2
Reliability	★★ 1/2
Parts/Service Availability	★★
Handling	★★★ 1/2
Engine Performance	★★ 1/2

Engine	twin cylinder, piston port, two-stroke
Bore & stroke	64x54 mm
Displacement	347 cc
Compression ratio	7.5:1
Bhp at rpm	36 at 7,000
Transmission	5 speed
Primary drive	gear
Clutch	multi-disc, wet plate
Brakes: front	twin-leading shoe, drum
Brakes: rear	single-leading shoe, drum
Tire size: front	3.00-18
Tire size: rear	3.50-18
Fuel capacity	3.2 gal
Wheelbase	52.8 in.
Weight	326 lb
Seat height	31.1 in.
Quarter-mile	15.49 sec at 81.08 mph*
Top Speed	95.31 mph*

Cycle World magazine test, June 1970

The R5 was Yamaha's new 350 for 1970. The styling of the R5 was very clean and clearly not influenced by the street scrambler styling of some of Yamaha's earlier bikes. The exhaust pipes ran low and parallel to the ground. The gas tank styling was very appealing and compared by some to the styling of the earlier Triumph 500 Trophy. The engine covers, cylinders, and head were finished in black with the engine cover's ridges and the exposed fin surfaces and edges were polished aluminum. The whole package was very appealing and purposeful in its look and one of Yamaha's most attractive bikes of the time.

The engine in the R5 was the typical, for the time, Yamaha twin-cylinder, piston-port two-stroke with oil-injection lubrication and a five-speed transmission. The engine was very similar to the YR2 engine

A 1972 R5C with its 347 cc engine. Other features included oil injection lubrication and a five-speed transmission. The engine was rated at 36 horsepower at 7,000 rpm. *Mark Witzerman*

that was brought out in 1967, which had only detail changes from the earlier YR1 engine. The bore and stroke for the R5 were changed slightly from the YR2 engine to shorten the stroke, resulting in a rather insignificant displacement decrease of 1 cc. Power output for both was rated at 36 horsepower at 7,000 rpm.

Changes to the R5 engine were more developmental refinements than any real leap forward. In addition to the difference in the power ratings, this is borne out by the results of the performance test for the two bikes. The June 1970 *Cycle World* test of the R5 showed performance figures of 15.49 seconds at 81.08 miles per hour for the quarter-mile and an actual top speed of 95.31 miles per hour. The quarter time for the YR2 tested by *Cycle World* in June of 1968 was only a little less than 0.2 of a second slower for the quarter-mile. The difference doesn't really indicate any performance improvement, since this difference in the quarter-mile times could easily be accounted for by the rider or the test conditions on the days the bikes were tested.

This is a Twin Jet 100 engine in a Rickman frame set up for racing. Rickman was a specialist frame builder operating in Massachusetts in the 1960s and 1970s. Special parts include gas tank, seat, clip-ons, and the very special triangular shaped racing tires. The large object under the bike is a stand to support the bike since the center stand has been removed for racing. This bike has been completely restored and never started. The owner appreciates the bike for its looks and has no intention of running the bike.

A 1971 XS1B with its attractive styling. The parallel twin engine had all of the appeal of a British 650 twin with the added sophistication of a single overhead cam. Quite different from other multi-cylinder Japanese bikes of the early 1970s, the Yamaha 650 was nonetheless very successful. *Yamaha Motor Corporation, USA*

The handling of the R5 was appropriate for what the bike was intended for. The tires and shocks performed well, but the handling was deemed to be a little too quick in *Cycle World's* test at the time, due to the bike's 52.8-inch wheelbase. (It's rather interesting to note that while the handling on the R5 was considered to be a little too quick when the bike was tested in 1970, that in *Cycle World's* 1973 test of the then new RD350, it was stated that the RD350 possessed the same excellent handling characteristics as the R5 that had been tested a few years earlier. I guess the pros and cons of quick handling are subject to the likes and dislikes of the rider and the times.)

Today the R5 is interesting as an example of early 1970s two-stroke technology. Not commonly seen, the R5 is nonetheless an attractive bike to this era's two-stroke enthusiast. Check the gas tank and tank emblems on any prospective R5. Tank emblems for this age of Yamaha are hard to find.

1970–1985, XS1, XS2, XS650 (654 cc)

Collectibility	★★★ 1/2
Passenger Accommodations	★★★
Reliability	★★★ 1/2
Parts/Service Availability	★★★★
Handling	★★ 1/2
Engine Performance	★★ 1/2

The 1979 XS650 when compared to the 1971 XS1B shows how little the 650 twin changed over eight years. Probably the most significant change is the front disc brake. Other changes include the upswept exhaust, angled-back instruments, and exposed rear shock springs. This Yamaha advertising photo points out the bike's significant features. *Yamaha Motor Corporation, USA*

Engine	vertical twin, four-stroke, single overhead cam
Bore & stroke	75 x 74 mm
Displacement	654 cc
Compression ratio	8.8:1
Bhp at rpm	53 at 7,000
Transmission	5 speed
Primary drive	gear
Clutch	multi disc, wet plate
Brakes: front	twin-leading-shoe drum
Brakes: rear	single-leading-shoe drum
Tire size: front	3.25-19
Tire size: rear	4.00-18
Fuel capacity	3.3 gal
Wheelbase	56.1 in.
Weight	428 lb
Seat height	31.8 in.
Quarter-mile	14.23 sec at 93.26 mph*
Top Speed	104.9 mph*

Cycle World magazine test, March 1970

With the introduction of the XS1, Yamaha entered into a new sector of the motorcycle market and a completely different concept in engine design. The XS1 engine was a 650 cc four-stroke parallel twin. At first, it is hard to understand why Yamaha chose this particular engine design. Honda had just recently introduced the CB750 with its inline four-cylinder engine, Kawasaki had introduced the H1 with its three-cylinder engines and even BSA, while still building twins, had produced the three-cylinder Rocket Three. So with the trend of the time being toward more cylinders and more complexity, Yamaha chose to equip its newest, largest displacement model to date with an engine that was a throwback to 20 years earlier. It's also rather interesting that Yamaha chose a 650 parallel twin, since the British manufacturers had been building 650 parallel twins well before Yamaha had started building motorcycles. The other Japanese manufacturers had decided to go around this section of the market, but Yamaha decided to go head to head with the British in a section of the market that the British clearly controlled.

This is a 1974 TX750. With the Honda Four and the Suzuki Triple engines setting the standard, the twin cylinder TX750 with its Omni-phase balancer bucked the trend. If you are looking for a bike that will attract attention with comments like, "I've never seen one of those before," then the TX750 is the bike for you. *Roger Cole*

There were advantages to a 650 twin. The design concept was well proven, and parallel twins had been popular with motorcyclists for many years. Also, the XS1 was definitely a Yamaha and as such was more sophisticated than the BSA or Triumph 650 twins of the time. The engine was overhead cam, primary drive was by gear, and the transmission was a five-speed. As an added bonus, the engine didn't leak oil.

The Yamaha had the sound and feel of a British twin, but there were some interesting differences. The XS1 had a light flywheel so when the throttle was twisted, the engine rpm picked up quickly. Care had to be taken, however, to keep the revs up and not select too high a gear or the engine would stumble. Also, the XS1 did not handle particularly well and the brakes were prone to fade when the bike was pushed.

Over the production run, numerous improvements were made and many variations of the XS1 were sold. The length of time that the XS1 and its variations continued to be built and sold by Yamaha confirms that this model has to be considered a success.

In hindsight, Yamaha made the right choice when it decided to build a 650 parallel twin. The XS1, in its many variations, remained in production and sold well for more than 15 years while the British motorcycle industry withered almost out of existence within 5 years of the XS1's introduction.

If you want a bike that is in many ways a throwback to an earlier time but yet is an excellent example of what Yamaha did to beat the British at their own game, a Yamaha 650 twin is a good choice. Couple this with a long production run, good availability, and high current popularity and the 650 twin is certainly an attractive bike. Yamaha 650 twins enjoyed a long production run, so most parts are available. Any bike being considered for purchase should be considered based on how much work the buyer is willing to do to bring the motorcycle up to the desired condition.

The Yamaha 650s are an interesting mix of a classic British motorcycle concept with Japanese styling and improvements. The first thing that strikes me is the appearance of the XS650. While there is no doubt that the Yamaha is a vertical twin, it does not look like a British twin. The XS650 exhibits a slight similarity to a Norton Commando, but there is no doubt that the Yamaha is Japanese and not British. Don't get me wrong—the Yamaha is a good-looking bike but the styling is definitely different than the British twins'.

The other thing that is apparent is something that is often mentioned when comparing Japanese bikes to British bikes—the Yamaha does not leak oil. While this may be a minor consideration to some people, it is something that I personally greatly appreciate. There is nothing more aggravating than going into the shed where I store my bikes and finding a puddle of oil under my BSA. To make matters worse, the BSA's leak can't be stopped; it's inherent in the design.

Starting the XS650 is far easier than kick-starting any of the British twins. With the XS650 you turn the key on and press the starter button. The starter turns the engine over for a couple of seconds, then the engine fires up. Very straightforward, no ceremony, no ritual, just a running engine.

With the engine started it's now time to take the XS650 for a ride. I get on the bike, pull away, and immediately notice that the Yamaha is very much a 650 vertical twin. To me the one thing that is always instantly noticeable on any twin of this size is the vibration. The Yamaha, although perhaps a bit smoother than a British twin, still vibrates.

Acceleration of the XS650 is brisk, though not as quick as, say, a Honda 750 of the same vintage. Handling seems reasonable for a mid-1970s motorcycle, although the reputation for the Yamahas is that they do not handle as well as a British bike. For the riding that I'm doing, though,

1972–1974, TX750 (743 cc)

Collectibility	★★★
Passenger Accommodations	★★★
Reliability	★
Parts/Service Availability	★
Handling	★★ 1/2
Engine Performance	★★ 1/2

Engine	parallel twin, four-stroke, single overhead cam
Bore & stroke	80x74 mm
Displacement	743 cc
Compression ratio	8.4:1
Bhp at rpm	n/a
Transmission	5 speed
Primary drive	straight cut gear
Clutch	multi disc, wet plate
Brakes: front	single disc
Brakes: rear	single-leading-shoe drum
Tire size: front	3.50H19
Tire size: rear	4.00H18
Fuel capacity	3.7 gal
Wheelbase	57.3 in.
Weight	518 lb
Seat height	31.0 in.
Quarter-mile	13.72 sec at 97.2 mph*
Top Speed	110 mph estimated*

*Cycle magazine test, March 1973

The TX750 is interesting and significant both for what Yamaha intended it to be and for what it actually turned out to be. As with the XS650, the TX750 had a twin-cylinder engine at a time when the trend was toward three- and four-cylinder engines. With the TX750, Yamaha planned to market a bike that could compete with the Honda and Kawasaki fours and at the same time the BSA, Triumph, Kawasaki, and Suzuki triples. The TX750 was to be a big bike with reasonably good performance but in a less complicated package. There would only be two spark plugs to change, two carburetors to balance, and two pistons, cylinders, and ring sets to maintain rather than the three or four associated with the more complicated multi-cylinder engines. Nevertheless, even with the simplicity, the key to success was to match the smoothness of the multi-cylinder engines. In order to achieve this, Yamaha used a dynamic balancing system that was referred to as the "Omni-Phase Balancer." What this was, essentially, was a shaft with bobweights that rotated in sync with the crankshaft to counteract the vibration induced by the vertical twin engine configuration.

Early Yamaha disc brake setups consisted of a single disc on the front with the caliper mounted on the front side of the fork tube. This right side view shows the TX750's substantial twin cylinder engine and the OHC750 markings on the side cover to differentiate it from less sophisticated vertical twins. *Roger Cole*

To a certain extent, Yamaha succeeded with the bike. The TX750 was well received by the motorcycling press. In the March 1973 Cycle magazine test, the TX750 was reported to be one of the world's ten quickest production bikes in the quarter-mile. The TX also handled reasonably well, but above all, the engine was smooth and there was very little vibration present when riding the bike. The Omni-Phase Balancer definitely did what it was intended to do.

On the other hand, there were the negatives. Although the bike was reasonably quick, it didn't break any new ground or set any records. Although the handling was adequate, it also did not set any new standards. All in all, the performance of the TX750 was not quite up to the highest standards of the day; but then again, it was a twin and it was smooth. If performance was the TX750's only problem, it may well have succeeded, particularly if it had been around long enough to be developed and its blandness overcome. However, there were a few major problems. The most significant of these was crankshaft failure. It was eventually determined that the crankshaft failures occurred because the balancing shafts that made up the Omni-Phase Balancing system were frothing the oil, causing oil starvation to the crankshaft bearings. The oil starvation problem with the early TX750s led to a reputation for self-destructing engines. Beyond this problem was the tendency for the balancing shafts to go out of sync when the chains driving the balancers stretched. The stretched chains caused the balancers to no longer do their intended job, which led to increased engine vibration. Yamaha eventually solved these problems, but by this time it was too late. The TX had developed a bad reputation, sales dwindled, and it was quickly withdrawn from the market.

So the appeal of the TX750 depends on how you view things. The early TX750s were not very reliable, which led to the bike being unpopular and withdrawn from production after a very short period of time. From this perspective the TX750 is not a very desirable bike. On the other hand, the short period of production and the low popularity of the bike have resulted in its being a very rare motorcycle. If you want a bike that will attract attention for its "what is it?" quality the TX750 certainly has to be considered. When buying a TX750 remember that these are rare bikes, and any parts that need to be replaced will be very difficult to find.

the handling does not present a problem. In addition to the handling, the braking is excellent with a nice feel to it.

The XS650's exhaust note is pleasant and sounds healthy as the bike accelerates. It does strike me, however, that the sound of a bike's exhaust is like its styling: It's a matter of what you like. Anyone that likes the sound of a vertical twin will like the sound of the Yamaha. More purposeful, some would say, than the sound of an inline four.

Seat comfort is about on par with any mid-1970s Japanese motorcycle, except maybe a Gold Wing. The seat is fine for around-town riding and the rides to a friend's house a couple of towns over, but not something that you would want to spend a lot of hours sitting on. You also have to factor in the vibration. If you were to spend the day on a Yamaha 650 and cover a lot of miles you'd certainly get a good nights sleep.

All in all the XS650 is just the thing if you want the character and simplicity of a vertical twin but want the technical innovation of a 1970s Yamaha. You get the sound, feel, and performance of a traditional, classic motorcycle without the problems associated with owning a Triumph, BSA, or any of the other classic British twins.

1973–1975, RD350 (347 cc)

In 1973 Yamaha introduced the RD350 with its reed valve induction and six-speed transmission. This was to be a very successful and popular model line that included the RD350, the RD400, and the RD400 Daytona Special. *Bob Shue*

Collectibility	★★★ 1/2
Passenger Accommodations	★★ 1/2
Reliability	★★★
Parts/Service Availability	★★★
Handling	★★★★
Engine Performance	★★★

Engine	twin cylinder, reed valve, two-stroke
Bore & stroke	64x54 mm
Displacement	347 cc
Compression ratio	6.6:1
Bhp at rpm	28.0 at 7,000
Transmission	6 speed
Primary drive	gear
Clutch	multi disc, wet plate
Brakes: front	single disc
Brakes: rear	drum
Tire size: front	3.00-18
Tire size: rear	3.50-18
Fuel capacity	3.2 gal
Wheelbase	52.5 in.
Weight	344 lb
Seat height	30.0 in.
Quarter-mile	14.3 sec at 89.8 mph*
Top Speed	99 mph*

Cycle World magazine test, February 1973

Subtle changes occurred over the RD350 model line. Here we have a 1975 RD350B showing the nice engine lines and the side cover 350 Torque Induction emblems. *Mark Witzerman*

The RD350 was in many ways very similar to its predecessor, the R5. The RD350 kept the best attributes of the R5 and added a few new ones of its own. Drivetrain improvements consisted of reed valve induction for the engine, which yielded increased horsepower, and a six-speed rather than five-speed transmission. With the same first gear and top gear ratios as the R5, the RD had an enjoyable close-ratio six-speed transmission. These engine and transmission improvements resulted in quicker acceleration, with the quarter-mile time improving by better than one second over the R5—the RD350 ran the quarter-mile in the mid 14s.

The RD350 chassis was very similar to the R5, which meant that the RD350 handled very well. The steering response was very precise or perhaps, depending on your viewpoint, very quick. The downside of the excellent chassis setup and handling was that the RD350 suspension was rather stiff, resulting in a less than plush ride. The RD350's braking was very good, benefiting from the use of a front disc brake. Overall through the mid-1970s, the RD350 outperformed all other bikes in its class, including the Suzuki GT380 and the Kawasaki S3.

The RD350 was produced for several years with very few changes. This lack of significant changes, together with the fact that many RD350s were raced with only minor modifications from stock, proved that Yamaha got the design right from the beginning. Eventually, the engine displacement was enlarged, resulting in the RD400, which subsequently led to the last of the air-cooled RDs, the much-coveted RD400 Daytona.

If you are looking for an air-cooled two-stroke that has great performance and is fun to ride, the RD350 is the perfect choice. Put this great performance together with the fact that RD350s are still reasonably priced and fairly easy to find, and the combination is hard to beat. RD350s are relatively easy to locate parts for, but nonetheless be sure to carefully check the condition of the exhaust and other cosmetics to avoid unanticipated cost in bringing your RD back to its original condition.

Another view of a beautiful 1975 RD350B. This one has the optional rear rack to increase the luggage-carrying capacity. *Mark Witzerman*

A left side view of the RD350B, showing the spoke wheels and nice lines. *Mark Witzerman*

A close-up of the 1975 RD350, showing the simple layout of the instruments with the speedometer on the left, the tachometer on the right, and a few warning lights. *Mark Witzerman*

1976–1979, XS750 (747 cc)

Collectibility	★★ 1/2
Passenger Accommodations	★★★
Reliability	★★★★
Parts/Service Availability	★★★
Handling	★★★
Engine Performance	★★★

Engine	three cylinder, four-stroke, dual overhead cam
Bore & stroke	68x68.6 mm
Displacement	747 cc
Compression ratio	8.5:1
Bhp at rpm	n/a
Transmission	5 speed, shaft final drive
Primary drive	Hi-Vo chain
Clutch	wet clutch
Brakes: front	dual disc, single piston caliper
Brakes: rear	single disc, single piston caliper
Tire size: front	3.25H19
Tire size: rear	4.00H18
Fuel capacity	4.5 gal
Wheelbase	57.7 in.
Weight	552 lb
Seat height	31.9 in.
Quarter-mile	*13.98 sec at 95.33 mph
Top Speed	n/a

Cycle magazine test, June 1976

The much coveted RD400 Daytona Special with its cast wheels and disc brakes. This bike is on display at the annual Vintage Japanese Motorcycle Show at the White Rose Motorcycle Club in Jefferson, Pennsylvania. *Owner, Frank Sammis*

The first year for the RD400 with its cast wheels and rear disc brake was 1976. By the mid-1970s two-stroke motorcycles were on the wane but the RD400 carried on, and in doing so made a name for itself. *Randy Hayes*

The XS750 was brought out during a time when the trend was toward inline transversely mounted four-cylinder engines. At this time, Honda had the four-cylinder CB750 and the CB550, Kawasaki the four-cylinder Z1, and within a year, Suzuki was to have the four-cylinder GS750, but Yamaha decided that the XS750 would use a three-cylinder engine. Maybe this decision was meant to attract attention, or maybe Yamaha thought it had a better idea, but for whatever the reason, the XS750 did not follow the trend of the time.

The XS750 was not Yamaha's first attempt at a 750 cc Sport Tourer. A few years earlier there had been the TX750, which had followed the XS650 vertical twin design concept but had counter-rotating balancing shafts in the engine that were designed to reduce engine vibration. The TX750 was not a success.

But with the XS750, Yamaha did have a successful Sport Tourer. When the bike was introduced various motorcycle magazines reported how wonderful it was. The Yamaha three-cylinder engine, unlike the Kawasaki or Triumph triples, was very smooth. The XS750 also had a very nice ride that was said to be in the same league as a BMW, which during the mid-1970s was never said about a Japanese motorcycle. Shaft drive was used so there was no need for adjusting and oiling a chain. There were also cast-aluminum wheels and self-canceling turn signals. As a total package, the XS750 was exactly what Yamaha intended: a very well designed, highly competent Sport Tourer.

The XS750 was produced from 1976 until 1979. In 1980, the engine was enlarged to 850 cc, perhaps as a response to the Suzuki shaft drive GS850. The 850 cc version was designated the XS850 and was produced until 1982. As with the XS750, the XS850 was a great Sport Tourer, just in a slightly larger size. The XS750/850s, although not seen for sale as often as a Honda CB750, are available with some looking and are usually very reasonably priced. The XS750 is a great bike for someone looking for late-1970s' styling in a well-executed Yamaha. Parts availability for XS750s and XS850s are reasonably good, but when buying either be sure to figure in the cost of replacing any missing or incorrect parts.

The paint scheme of the RD400 Daytona Special was very simple and attractive. White paint with gold lettering and a blacked-out engine with polished engine fin edges. A very quick and impressive motorcycle. *Owner, Frank Sammis*

1978–1981, XS11 (1,102 cc)

Collectibility	★★★ 1/2
Passenger Accommodations	★★★★
Reliability	★★★★
Parts/Service Availability	★★★
Handling	★★★
Engine Performance	★★★★ 1/2

Engine	inline four, four-stroke, dual overhead cam
Bore & stroke	71.5 x 68.6 mm
Displacement	1,102 cc
Compression ratio	9.2:1
Bhp at rpm	n/a
Transmission	5 speed, shaft final drive
Primary drive	Hi-Vo chain and gear
Clutch	wet clutch
Brakes: front	dual disc with single piston calipers
Brakes: rear	single disc with single piston calipers
Tire size: front	3.50H19
Tire size: rear	4.50H17
Fuel capacity	5.2 gal
Wheelbase	60.8 in.
Weight	602 lb
Seat height	31.8 in.
Quarter-mile	11.82 sec at 115.38 mph*
Top Speed	124.7 mph*

Cycle magazine test, January 1978

Following the end of the RD400 in 1979, the Yamaha two-stroke street bike made its last appearance in 1984 as the RZ350. This is the Kenny Roberts Special. *Yamaha Motor Corporation, USA*

In addition to 350 cc and 400 cc displacement, the RD series also came in a 250 cc size. This is a 1975 RD250, displaying the same great looks as its larger sibling. *Perry Ritter*

The XS750 was one of the best Sport Tourers of the mid- to late 1970s, with its smooth three-cylinder engine, shaft drive, and comfortable ride. *James Townsend*

With the Yamaha three-into-one replacement exhaust, it is possible to get a nice view of the XS750 shaft drive setup and cast rear wheel. Up until the mid-1970s shaft drive was not common on Japanese motorcycles. With the introduction of bikes like the XS750 and the Suzuki GS850, shaft drive became recognized as a very desirable feature for a Sport Tourer. *James Townsend*

With the introduction of the XS11 in 1978, Yamaha dethroned the Kawasaki KZ1000 as the King of the Superbikes. The XS11 was by far the quickest production bike through the quarter-mile, with times consistently under 12 seconds.

The XS11 was different, though. Along with the blistering acceleration came civility, something that was not common in fast bikes in the 1970s. The engine in the XS11 was a dual overhead cam inline four-cylinder, which was pretty much the standard engine configuration for large displacement Japanese motorcycles of the time. The coil ignition was magnetically triggered and featured vacuum advance. The drivetrain was a five-speed transmission with shaft final drive. The excellent braking system—absolutely necessary considering the speed capability and weight of the XS11—featured dual discs in the front and a single disc in the rear. The dry weight of the bike was a little over 600 pounds. The wheelbase was over 60 inches. The XS11 was definitely a very big, very fast motorcycle.

Because of the long wheelbase and the suspension setup, the XS11 rode very nicely. By some accounts, the ride of the XS11 was equivalent to the ride of the Honda Gold Wing, which was certainly a high standard of comparison for ride quality. On the other hand, the XS11 did not handle very well. The long wheelbase that helped the smoothness of the ride did nothing for the responsiveness of the steering. The bike did not like to change lines in a corner, and with the power that was available it was possible to quickly find yourself in a scary situation if too much throttle was applied. The XS11 essentially consisted of excellent new engine technology with old, poor suspension technology.

In 1979, following in the mold of the XS650 and XS750 Specials, Yamaha introduced the XS11 Special. The Special offered a mildly leaned-back riding position; a smaller teardrop-shaped gas tank; higher, pulled-back handlebars; a stepped "Queen and King" seat; and a wide 16-inch rear tire. All of this, together with more chrome than the Standard XS11, gave the Special an appearance that many buyers found appealing.

Along with the styling differences, Yamaha made changes that improved the handling of the XS11 Special over that of the Standard. As Suzuki had done with a few of its models, Yamaha fitted the front end of the XS11 Special with adjustable air forks. The rear suspension of the Special was also improved with shock absorbers that had adjustable dampening in addition to the standard spring preload adjustment.

So the XS11 Standard is desirable in that it was the quickest bike of its day. With the XS11 Special, you have not only a very quick bike but also one of the early examples of a Japanese cruiser. Both bikes are desirable and can be found with a little searching, so the choice depends on which styling is more to your liking. Be sure to check any XS11 that you plan to buy for the condition of its exhaust and other cosmetics to avoid unplanned additional expenses.

The 1978 XS1100 with its 1,102 cc engine was very fast, and with its long wheelbase and suspension setup, it was also comfortable. This is an XS1100 Standard with its conventional styling and flat seat. *Yamaha Motor Corporation, USA*

1981–1997, Virago (748 cc)

Collectibility ★★★
Passenger Accommodations ★★★
Reliability ★★★★
Parts/Service Availability ★★★★ 1/2
Handling ★★★
Engine Performance ★★★

Engine	75 degree V-twin, four-stroke, air cooled, chain driven single overhead camshafts
Bore & stroke	83.0 x 69.2 mm
Displacement	748 cc
Compression ratio	8.7:1
Bhp at rpm	60 at 7,000 claimed
Transmission	5 speed
Primary drive	straight cut gear
Clutch	wet clutch
Brakes: front	single disc
Brakes: rear	single-leading-shoe drum
Tire size: front	3.50H 9
Tire size: rear	130/90 -16
Fuel capacity	3.8 gal
Wheelbase	60.0 in.
Weight	502 lb
Seat height	28.0 in.
Quarter-mile	13.44 sec at 98.68 mph*
Top Speed	104.1 mph calculated*

*Cycle magazine test, June 1981

Yamaha's earlier success with Specials led to the Midnight Specials of the early 1980s. The XS11 Midnight Special was functionally the same as the regular XS11 Special—stepped seat, pull-back bars, short exhaust, and overall cruiser styling—but the whole package was finished in black and gold. In addition to the things like gas tank and fenders that you would expect to be black, there were black carburetors, horns, handlebars, fork tubes, and exhaust. All the highlights were then finished in gold. This is a 1981 XS11 Midnight Special. *Charles Wildman*

Following the success of the XS750 Special in the late 1970s and the XS11 Special in 1980, Yamaha was confident that the time was right for the ultimate Special. This would be a bike that would have the cruiser looks that made the previous Specials so successful. This time, the bike would also have the engine to go with the looks, a 750 cc V-twin. Comparisons with Harley-Davidson were immediately drawn, but the Virago was not an H-D copy. Yes, the engine was a V-twin, but there were many significant differences. The cylinders were set at 75 degrees, and the rear cylinder was offset 24 millimeters to the left of the centerline of the front cylinder to improve rear cylinder cooling. There was a single overhead camshaft for each cylinder, and the air intake was through the stamped steel backbone of the frame. In addition to the V-twin engine, the first Virago also had shaft drive and a monoshock rear end. It was definitely a V-twin cruiser but certainly not a copy of a Harley. Acceleration was not as quick as many 750s of the time, but the engine was very flexible, with plenty of torque, and it suited the role of the bike very well.

Here you can see the detail of the front end of the XS11 Midnight Special. The black fender, fork tubes, exhaust, horn, and engine are all visible. The front forks are leading axle to allow more suspension travel. Brakes are dual disc with slotted rotors. *Charles Wildman*

The XS11 Midnight Special had the same stepped seat and short mufflers as other Yamaha Specials, but with the black engine and exhaust and gold highlights the Midnight Special was indeed something special to look at. *Charles Wildman*

The rider's view of an XS11 Midnight Special, showing the black handlebars and turn signals. The instrument layout is typical early 1980s with equal-sized, separate tachometer and speedometer with indicator lights for the turn signals, oil pressure, and headlamp in the center pod. Additional indicator lights for neutral, high beam, and low fuel were located in the bottom of the tachometer. *Charles Wildman*

The XV750 went through a few changes over the years. In 1984 the air intake system was changed and the air filters moved to the side of the engine. The original monoshock rear suspension was dropped in favor of a more traditional twin shock rear end. In 1984, the tariff-beater version of the Virago came into being. Like nearly all 750 cc Japanese motorcycles of the day, the displacement of the Virago was reduced to 699 cc to slide in under the 700 cc tariff limit. In 1988 when the tariff ended, the Virago returned to its 750 cc displacement. Beyond this, the 750 cc Virago remained essentially unchanged for the next ten years.

Yamaha wasn't satisfied with having just one XV model, and shortly after the XV750 was in the showrooms, the XV920 was introduced. The XV920 was aimed at the European sports touring market, so the seating position and styling were appropriately different than the XV750's. The seat had less of a step to it, the handlebars were a little lower, and the footpegs were positioned farther back to give the appropriate sport touring seating position. For styling, the gas tank was a more functional shape and size, and the mufflers were longer rather than the chopped off cruiser style. The engine of the 920 was essentially a bored-out version of the 750 engine, with the engine bore going from 83 millimeters to 92 millimeters and the stroke staying at 69.2 millimeters. The other differences between the two Viragos were the final drive and the brakes. The XV920 had a fully enclosed chain final drive and dual disc front brakes, while the XV750s had shaft drive and single disc front brake.

Introduced in 1980 the Virago was the successor to the XS750 and XS11 Specials. With its V-twin engine, it was the ultimate cruiser of the day. This is a 1982 model. *Yamaha Motor Corporation, USA*

In 1984, the engine on the XV920 was enlarged to 1,000 cc and renamed the XV1000 Virago. In 1986 the displacement was increased again, to 1,100 cc, creating the XV1100 Virago. To round things out, in 1983 Yamaha introduced a smaller version of the Virago, the VX500. Although there were some technical differences in the execution, the XV500 maintained the Virago concept, a stylish V-twin powered cruiser. In 1987 the XV500 received a displacement increase to 535 cc. At this time, the XV535 is still currently in production.

The Virago has been a very popular bike for Yamaha. As I write this, the XV1100 and the XV535 are still part of Yamaha's lineup, and the XV750 was only discontinued in 1997. The Viragos are definitely classics but with two models still in production and very good availability, only time will tell if they become true collectibles. The best size Virago to buy depends on the preferences of the buyer; however, the larger displacement Viragos tend to be more desirable. Be sure to account for the cost to replace any damaged or missing parts on any Virago that you consider buying.

1982–1983, Seca Turbo (653 cc)

Collectibility	★★★★
Passenger Accommodations	★★★
Reliability	★★★
Parts/Service Availability	★★★
Handling	★★★
Engine Performance	★★★

Engine	transverse four, four-stroke, dual chain driven overhead cams, turbo charged 7.7 psi max.
Bore & stroke	63.0 x 52.4 mm
Displacement	653 cc
Compression ratio	8.2:1
Bhp at rpm	n/a
Transmission	5 speed
Primary drive	straight cut gear
Clutch	wet clutch
Brakes: front	dual disc, single piston calipers
Brakes: rear	single-leading-shoe drum
Tire size: front	3.25V19
Tire size: rear	120/90V18
Fuel capacity	4.1 gal
Wheelbase	56.7 in.
Weight	567 lb
Seat height	31.3 in.
Quarter-mile	12.49 sec at 105.63 mph*
Top Speed	128 mph calculated*

*Cycle magazine test, August 1982

The Seca 650 Turbo was Yamaha's entry into the Turbo wars. Attractive styling and the promise of a turbocharged engine made the Seca Turbo a very appealing motorcycle. Like all Turbos, the Seca was short-lived, available only in 1982 and 1983. *Yamaha Motor Corporation, USA*

The Yamaha Seca Turbo was introduced not long after the Honda CX500 Turbo. Yamaha, like Honda and, shortly thereafter, Suzuki and Kawasaki, viewed turbocharged motorcycles as the wave of the future. The Yamaha turbo was different in several respects from the Honda Turbo. The Yamaha engine was a 650 cc, inline, air-cooled four-cylinder as compared to the V-twin water-cooled 500 cc Honda. (Honda increased the displacement on its turbo to 650 cc the following year.) Where Honda had used digital fuel injection, the Yamaha used four carburetors. The carburetors were downstream from the turbo, so that the turbocharger pressurized the carburetors. At this time turbocharging was still a new phenomenon for production motorcycles and Yamaha's design was as good as Honda's, since no one particular configuration was considered to be better than another.

The Seca Turbo was developed from the normally aspirated Seca 650. Due to the addition of the turbocharger and related hardware, the Turbo ended up being about 75 pounds heavier than the non-turbo Seca. Since the Turbo used the same frame as the regular Seca, the result was less than spectacular handling. In addition, the Turbo was only slightly quicker accelerating than the regular Seca. To top off these disappointments, the Seca Turbo was proved in a test by *Cycle* magazine to definitely not be as fast as the Honda CX500 Turbo.

In 1983, Yamaha made several changes to the Turbo to improve performance. The weak acceleration performance was due in part to the low maximum boost pressure that Yamaha chose. In the 1982 Turbos, the wastegate had been set to limit boost pressure to a lowly maximum of 7 psi. In 1983 a stronger wastegate spring was installed and the muffler was modified to increase back pressure. The changes resulted in an increase in maximum boost pressure from the previous year's 7 psi to a more power producing 12 psi. Yamaha made these improvements available free of charge to all owners of the first-year turbos.

The final year for the Seca Turbo was 1983. In order to get the last of the Turbos off the showroom floor, Yamaha cut the price of the bike by 30 percent or more. Still, the bikes were slow to sell.

The Seca Turbo was manufactured for only two years. Yamaha, like the other Japanese motorcycle manufacturers, quickly came to the conclusion that the problems associated with turbocharging outweighed the benefits. This short life, together with slow sales, brought an end to the Yamaha Turbo and currently makes the bikes very difficult to find. Because of the short production run, parts for Seca Turbos that are unique to the model can be very hard to find. Additionally, if the turbocharger fails and has to be replaced, it is usually very expensive.

While the Seca Turbo is probably the least prized of all of the factory turbos, it is nonetheless an appealing item. Not only was the Seca Turbo made for only two years, but turbocharged motorcycles in general are very uncommon. Put the interesting idiosyncrasies of riding a turbocharged motorcycle together with its attention-grabbing, conversation-generating engine configuration and you have a very desirable motorcycle.

Future collectibles
1985–Present, V-Max (1,198 cc)

Collectibility	★★★
Passenger Accommodations	★★★
Reliability	★★★★
Parts/Service Availability	★★★★ 1/2
Handling	★★★
Engine Performance	★★★★★

Engine	70 degree V-four, four-stroke, liquid cooled, dual chain driven overhead camshafts
Bore & stroke	76.0x66.0 mm
Displacement	1,198 cc
Compression ratio	10.5:1
Bhp at rpm	119.08 at 9,000
Transmission	5 speed
Primary drive	spur gear
Clutch	wet clutch
Brakes: front	dual disc, dual piston calipers
Brakes: rear	single disc, dual piston calipers
Tire size: front	110/90V18
Tire size: rear	150/90V15
Fuel capacity	4.0 gal
Wheelbase	62.6 in.
Weight	618.5 lb
Seat height	30.5 in.
Quarter-mile	10.99 sec at 124.04 mph*
Top Speed	149 calculated*

Cycle magazine test, May 1985

The hot rod of motorcycles, the V-Max, first went on sale in 1985. The concept for the V-Max was very straightforward: eye-catching styling and brutal power. The large physical size of the engine, exhaust, and rear tire, combined with the stylized nonfunctional air scoops, a very small gas tank, and a seat shaped so that you couldn't slide off, made sure the V-Max *looked* fast as well. As impressive as the appearance was, the V-Max more than backed it up when it came to power. The engine was a dual overhead cam, 16-valve, liquid-cooled, four-stroke, V-four displacing just shy of 1,200 cc and producing 119 tire-smoking horsepower—a very impressive engine to back up the attention-grabbing appearance. But to top it off, and this certainly doesn't always happen, the V-Max did exactly what the looks and spec sheet said it should do, it was very quick. Typical quarter-mile times, recorded in magazine tests such as *Cycle's* May 1985 test on the V-Max, were in the high 10-second bracket, with terminal speeds of over 120 miles per hour. A very quick motorcycle, indeed.

The big, muscle-bound V-Max. While its styling was somewhat unconventional, there was no doubting what the V-Max was made for and what its strong point was. Its 1,198 cc V-4 engine made the V-Max one of the quickest bikes on the market. While not for everyone, the V-Max is desirable for the image it portrays and for having the muscle to back it up. This is from a 1987 Yamaha ad for the V-Max, highlighting the bike's best features. *Yamaha Motor Corporation, USA*

The engine in the V-Max was a hopped-up version of that of Yamaha's touring bike, the Venture. The V-Max engine gained its extra power through several well-proven hop-up techniques. The valves were larger, valve stems were smaller diameter, cams had more lift and overlap, pistons were lightened, and the carburetors were larger.

The most interesting thing about the V-Max was the complex intake manifold system dubbed V-Boost. The V-Boost system was a series of passages and solenoid-actuated valves that progressively enabled each cylinder to draw through a pair of carburetors as the engine speed increased. At low rpm, each cylinder had its own individual carburetor. By the time the engine reached 8,000 rpm, each cylinder was drawing through not only its own carburetor but also through the carburetor of the adjacent cylinder. The V-Boost system gave the V-Max plenty of low and midrange torque with tons of power at the top end of the engine's rev range. The one negative aspect of the V-Max was its handling. While building a reputation as being almost unbeatable in a straight line by other unmodified motorcycles, it also developed a reputation as having poor handling. Most of the problems had to do with front-end shake at high speed, and this affected all production years. Various fixes have been developed for this problem over the years and most that I've seen are very straightforward to implement, such as tire selection or changing hardware stackup in the steering stem.

As I write this, the V-Max is still in production, essentially unchanged in almost 15 years. The V-Max's collectibility is unproven at this time, but history shows that fast bikes, even those with less than perfect handling (i.e., Kawasaki's H2), attract the attention of collectors. When buying a V-Max be sure the motorcycle has been properly maintained and that it is in good running order. V-Maxs tend to be driven hard and require proper maintenance to avoid mechanical problems.

1985–1988, FZ750 (749 cc)

Collectibility	★★★
Passenger Accommodations	★★★
Reliability	★★★★
Parts/Service Availability	★★★★
Handling	★★★★★
Engine Performance	★★★★

Engine	transverse four cylinder, four-stroke, liquid cooled, dual chain driven overhead camshafts
Bore & stroke	68.0x51.6 mm
Displacement	749 cc
Compression ratio	11.2:1
Bhp at rpm	85.33 at 11,500
Transmission	6 speed
Primary drive	straight cut gear

1985–1988, FZ750 (749 cc)   (continued)

Clutch	wet clutch
Brakes: front	dual disc, dual piston calipers
Brakes: rear	single disc, single piston caliper
Tire size: front	120/80V16
Tire size: rear	130/80V18
Fuel capacity	6.1 gal
Wheelbase	58.5 in.
Weight	524.5 lb
Seat height	31.3 in.
Quarter-mile	11.31 sec at 116.37mph*
Top Speed	148 mph calculated*

*Cycle magazine test, February 1986

The FZ750 came onto the scene in 1985 at a time when the differences between sport bikes, cruisers, and touring bikes were becoming very distinct. During this time, the FZ750 was one of the bikes that made a clear definition of what a sport bike was. Performance of the FZ750 was stunning, and many touted it as a giant leap forward.

A large part of the bike's advancement lay in its engine. The engine was a liquid-cooled, inline four, producing 85 horsepower. The engine had several interesting features, with the most notable being the Yamaha-designed five-valve head. This cylinder head design allowed for an 11.2:1 compression ratio, which was a very high compression ratio for the time. This configuration became known as the Yamaha Genesis engine. The FZ750 cylinders were tilted forward at a 45-degree angle, allowing the bike to be designed with more weight on the front wheels. The forward slant of the cylinders also allowed the air box to be situated directly above the engine in space normally occupied by the front of the gas tank. This allowed the gas tank to extend back into the area normally occupied by the air box. This swapping of locations between the air box and the fuel tank accomplished two things. First, since the fuel was now carried in a more central location there was less change in the weight distribution as the fuel was used. Secondly, the air box was better situated to take in unheated air.

The FZ750 was very quick, with a quarter-mile time in the low 11s and top speed of just a few miles per hour short of 150. Handling was very good, particularly if the stock tires were replaced.

The FZ750 was the top of the sporting bike pile for about a year until the introduction of the Suzuki GSX-R 750. It was not that the Suzuki was so much better than the Yamaha; it was more that Yamaha was not going to go unchallenged in the sport bike market. The FZ750 was a significant bike, is often seen for sale, and has almost guaranteed collectibility. When buying an FZ750 check the condition of the fairing, the exhaust, and other cosmetic items. Be sure to check details such as fairing fasteners, decals, and the windscreen. These are minor items, but the cost can add up if a large number of them need to be replaced.

The 1985 FZ750 was a significant advancement for sporting bikes and for about a year was the best sporting bike available. Future collectibility of the FZ750 is almost a sure thing. *Yamaha Motor Corporation, USA*

Chapter 5

Other Manufacturers

MODELS COVERED

Bridgestone Sport 90
Bridgestone 175 Dual Twin
Bridgestone 350 GTR
Lilac LS-18
Marusho Magnum
Tohatsu Runpet Sport CA-2
Tohatsu LD-3

In addition to the Big Four, there have been, as you may well imagine, numerous other motorcycle manufacturers in Japan. Some, such as Meguro, which was absorbed by Kawasaki, have ceased to exist. Many, like Cabton and Meihatu, never made it to the U.S market. Others, like Pointer and Yamaguchi, are obscure enough that very few people even know that they were once available in the United States. Still others, like

A beautiful example of a Bridgestone Sport90 with the half-chrome gas tank and the high output 8.8 horsepower engine. *Motorcycle owned/restored by Gary Toomer; photo by Hal Toomer*

This is a 1966 Bridgestone Hurricane Scrambler (HS175) showing the high-level exhaust with the very cool stingers. Note the interesting intake setup with the air filter canister feeding air through the rubber and chrome tubes to the carburetors under the engine side covers. *Motorcycle owned/restored by Gary Toomer; photo by Hal Toomer*

Tohatsu and Lilac, were available only for a short period of time. Then there was Bridgestone, which was far more successful than the other manufacturers in this chapter at designing and building motorcycles. In the end, however, after what is rumored to be not-so-gentle persuasion by other major manufacturers, Bridgestone moved on to other endeavors. Unfortunately for us, only a handful of bikes from any of these other manufacturers ever made it to our shores. In this chapter, we will look at some of the more obscure and lesser-known of the classic Japanese motorcycles.

Bridgestone

Shojiro Ishibashi founded Bridgestone Tire Company Limited in 1931 in the city of Kurume to manufacture tires. The Bridgestone name is a variation of the English translation (stone bridge) of the name Ishibashi. In 1952, Bridgestone entered into the powered two-wheeled vehicle business by attaching motors, purchased from the Prince Motor Co., to the rear wheel of the bicycles that it had been building since the late 1940s. By the late 1950s Bridgestone was building small, fan-cooled, two-stroke 50 cc two-speed motorcycles. Exports of Bridgestone motorcycles to the United States started in 1963 through an agreement with Rockford Motors of Rockford, Illinois. In 1964, Bridgestone introduced the 90 Sport, and by 1968, the line had been expanded to include a 50 Sport, a 50 Step-thru, a 60 Sport, four variations of the 90, two variations of the 100, the 175 Dual Twin, 175 Hurricane Scrambler, and the 100 and 175 Racers. This was also the year that Bridgestone introduced the 350 cc rotary-valve, six-speed, two-stroke GTR. In 1970 Bridgestone added the street scrambler version of the 350, the GTO, to its lineup. Even with all this success, by 1973 Bridgestone had quit producing motorcycles using the Bridgestone name supposedly due to pressure from Honda, Suzuki, and Yamaha, who were all major OEM customers for Bridgestone tires.

1964–1967, Bridgestone 90 (88 cc)

Collectibility	★★
Passenger Accommodations	★
Reliability	★★
Parts/Service Availability	★
Handling	★
Engine Performance	★

Engine	single cylinder, rotary valve, two-stroke
Bore & stroke	50x45 mm
Displacement	88 cc
Compression ratio	6.55:1
Bhp at rpm	8.8 at 8,000
Transmission	4 speed
Primary drive	gear
Clutch	multi disc, wet plate
Brakes: front	single-leading-shoe drum
Brakes: rear	single-leading-shoe drum
Tire size: front	2.50x18
Tire size: rear	2.75x18
Fuel capacity	2.64 gal
Wheelbase	48.6 in.
Weight	271 lb
Seat height	30.7 in.
Quarter-mile	n/a
Top Speed	65 mph (claimed)

A Bridgestone ad for the Dual Twin. The images in the background always made me want to run right out and buy one. *Bridgestone.*

The single-cylinder Bridgestone 90s have one of the most desirable features of larger displacement Bridgestone motorcycles: the two-stroke, rotary-valve engine. This engine configuration yielded an impressive 8.8 horsepower for the 90 Sport and 7.8 horsepower for the other models of the Bridgestone 90s. The transmission for all models was a four-speed with a rotary shift pattern. Bridgestone claimed a top speed for the 90 Sport of a little over 65 miles per hour.

The 90s were offered in four different versions: Sport, Deluxe, Mountain, and Trail. The Sport was the quickest of the group, with the high output motor, and the most stylish with its uniquely shaped half-chrome gas tank. Other than the lower power output for the other 90s, most other model differences were cosmetic in nature. The Deluxe was similar to the Sport except for the gas tank shape and paint scheme. The Trail, fitted with the low-level exhaust of the street models and similar in appearance to the Deluxe, offered quick-change dual rear sprockets

Bridgestone advertising often used very stylishly dressed ladies to enhance the visual appeal of the motorcycles. This is the cover of a Bridgestone sales brochure with one of these stylish ladies obviously ready to go for a ride. The bike is a 100 TMX. *Bridgestone*

and dual-purpose tires. The Mountain was the most distinct of the 90s, offering high-level exhaust, cross-braced handlebars, solo seat, engine crash guards, and a front fender mud flap as well as the quick change dual rear sprockets.

The Bridgestone 90 is an ideal bike for someone looking for something out of the ordinary in a small displacement motorcycle; however, Bridgestone 90s in any of the model variations are quite scarce and seldom seen for sale. Bridgestone parts are difficult to find, so be sure that any Bridgestone 90 you buy is complete and in good running order.

1965–1968, Bridgestone 175s (177 cc)

Collectibility	★★
Passenger Accommodations	★★
Reliability	★★
Parts/Service Availability	★
Handling	★
Engine Performance	★ 1/2

Engine	twin cylinder, rotary valve, two-stroke
Bore & stroke	50x45 mm
Displacement	177 cc
Compression ratio	9.5:1
Bhp at rpm	20 at 8,000
Transmission	selectable - 5 speed or rotary shift 4 speed
Primary drive	helical gear
Clutch	multi disc, wet plate
Brakes: front	twin-leading-shoe drum
Brakes: rear	single-leading-shoe drum
Tire size: front	2.50x18
Tire size: rear	2.75x18
Fuel capacity	2.6 gal
Wheelbase	48.6 in.
Weight	282 lb
Seat height	31.0 in.
Quarter-mile	17.8 sec at 72 mph*
Top Speed	81 mph*

*Cycle World magazine test, February 1966

The two versions of the Bridgestone 175, the Dual Twin and the Hurricane Scrambler, were essentially the same motorcycle. The engine was a rotary-valve two-stroke twin, displacing 177 cc. As with the 350s, the carburetors were positioned under the engine side covers with the air intake coming through an air filter behind the engine in the space normally occupied by the carburetors on most bikes. The air passed from an air filter canister through rubber tubes on each side of the canister, then through chromed metal tubes, and finally through rubber tubes

Rotary Transmissions

The Dual Twin gets its name from its unique transmission. With the flip of a small lever on the side of the engine, you had a choice of a five-speed transmission or a rotary four-speed. In the five-speed position, the transmission was a normal five-speed. Neutral was at the top, with the other four gears being consecutively selected by pressing down on the shift lever. With the little lever flipped to the rotary position, the transmission became a four-speed rotary shift. If you have never driven a rotary transmission, this could turn out to be a little unnerving. The shift pattern started with neutral at the top, then by pressing down the shift lever you consecutively selected the next three gears. What was unique was that if you were in fourth gear and pressed down again, you ended up selecting neutral.

The theory for this shift pattern was that if you were traveling down the road in fourth gear and came to a stop, you did not have to shift down through the gears to reach neutral but could simply press down on the shift lever once and be in neutral. From there, the four gears could again be selected by continuing to press down on the lever. The problem—perhaps disastrous—with a rotary shift pattern is that if you are in fourth gear at speed, then forget what gear you are in and press down on the shift lever to select the next higher gear, you will find yourself in neutral. If you are then inattentive enough to press down again in hopes of once again getting power to the rear wheel you will find yourself in first gear. While this may be nothing more than exciting on a bike like the Bridgestone Dual Twin, a rotary transmission on a larger bike like a Honda Dream Sport could be disastrous. Needless to say, rotary transmissions fell out of favor in the late 1960s.

The best of the Bridgestones, a 350 GTR, with the rotary valve engine, six-speed transmission, dry clutch, non-slip seat, and beautiful styling. *Motorcycle owned/restored by Gary Toomer; photo by Hal Toomer*

again to get to the engine side covers, where the carburetors were located. All this air intake plumbing gave the 175s a rather interesting appearance.

Suspension on the bikes was telescopic front forks and dual-shock swingarm in the rear with drum brakes both front and rear. The dual mode transmission was very interesting in that it was selectable, being either a five- or four-speed rotary, and was what gave the Dual Twin its name.

The difference between the Dual Twin and the Hurricane Scrambler was mainly cosmetic. The Dual Twin was the street version of the 175 with a low-level exhaust and slightly lower handlebars. The Hurricane Scrambler had higher handlebars with a crossbrace and the obligatory street scrambler high exhaust. In addition, there was also a skid plate under the engine. The Hurricane Scrambler also shared the suedelike seat top with the 350GTR. Other than these cosmetic differences, the two 175s were very much the same.

While more common than the Bridgestone 90s, the 175s are still fairly scarce and will require the person who wants to add one to his collection to do some searching. Check the chrome carefully on any Bridgestone 175 that you consider buying. The gas tank chrome, particularly, is not very good and is subject to bubbling and peeling.

1968–1971, 350 GTR (345 cc)

Collectibility	★★★
Passenger Accommodations	★★ 1/2
Reliability	★★
Parts/Service Availability	★
Handling	★★ 1/2
Engine Performance	★★ 1/2

Engine	twin cylinder, rotary valve, two-stroke
Bore & stroke	61x59 mm
Displacement	345 cc
Compression ratio	9.3:1
Bhp at rpm	37 at 7,500
Transmission	6 speed
Primary drive	gear
Clutch	multi disc, wet plate
Brakes: front	twin-leading-shoe drum
Brakes: rear	single-leading-shoe drum
Tire size: front	3.25x19
Tire size: rear	3.25x19
Fuel capacity	3.8 gal
Wheelbase	54.1 in.
Weight	362 lb
Seat height	32.2 in.
Quarter-mile	14.3 sec at 93 mph*
Top Speed	104 mph*

*Cycle magazine test, August 1967

Introduced in 1968, the 350 GTR turned out to be Bridgestone's most impressive motorcycle. The specifications for the GTR sounded more like they belonged to a racer than to a street bike. In addition, the bike had many interesting and some rather unique features. In a *Cycle* magazine road test dated August 1967, the publication referred to the GTR as "An enthusiast's dream; a motorcyclist's motorcycle."

The GTR engine, although similar to previous Bridgestone engines, was newly designed, not just a revamped, enlarged displacement version of a smaller engine. Like the smaller Bridgestones, the GTR engine used rotary valves to accurately control the timing and duration of the fuel intake. The use of rotary valves led to the engine having a rather unusual appearance, since the carburetors were located under the engine side covers, while behind the cylinders, in the space usually filled by carburetors on most engines, was an oddly shaped air intake manifold. In addition to the rotary valves, the engine had chromed cylinder bores and was coupled to a six-speed transmission through a dry clutch.

In addition to the drivetrain, the GTR had other interesting features. The rear shocks had two positions for the upper mounts. The rear mounting position placed the shocks in an upright position and offered a firmer, more sporting ride. The forward mounting position placed the shocks at an angle, giving a softer, more comfortable ride. The shifter shaft and the rear brake shaft were exposed on both sides of the bike, allowing the shift pedal and the rear brake pedal to be mounted on either side. This allowed riders more accustomed to riding British bikes to have the dealer mount the shift lever on the right and the brake pedal on the left. The seat was interesting in that the top surface of it was a suedelike fuzz. In addition to having an unusual appearance, the seat was very functional, keeping you from sliding back hard acceleration. There was also the fifth gear indicator via a light in the speedometer that indicated when the transmission was in fifth with one more gear to go. A little strange when you first ride the bike, but it's something that turns out to be very useful when you become accustomed to it.

Riding the GTR is a unique experience. The bike sits high and is quite narrow. The feel is definitely more substantial than most 350s. A well-tuned GTR will

The second variation of the Bridgestone 350 was the GTO. The GTO was very similar to the GTR but with high-level exhaust, a shorter front fender with a mudflap, and braced handlebars. Again, a very stylish motorcycle. *Motorcycle owned/restored by Gary Toomer; photo by Hal Toomer*

Another stylish lady helping to sell a Bridgestone, in this case a 1970 350 GTO. *Bridgestone*

A July 1961 advertisement from *Motorcyclist* magazine explaining the enhancements of the 'Improved LS-18.' Note, too, the invitation to dealers to write for information. *Lilac*

A right side of a Lilac LS-18, showing the 250 cc V-twin engine. Also shown is the shaft drive used on almost all Lilacs and Marushos. *Lilac*

Several models of Lilac were imported in addition to the LS-18. This is Ralph Walker's CF-40, authentic except for a missing side cover. The engine is the typical Lilac V-twin, in this configuration displacing 125 cc and producing 10.5 horsepower. *Ralph Walker*

always start on the first or second second kick, or on a bad day, the third. This applies whether the bike has been sitting for five minutes or has been properly stored for several months. The bike accelerates briskly and represents the best in late 1960s two-stroke technology. Six speeds to shift through and a nice cloud of smoke behind you.

The Bridgestone GTR and the similar GTO street Scrambler with its high handlebars and high-level exhaust are both interesting and desirable motorcycles. Today, the GTR and the GTO are both rather rare, with the GTO being rarer. When buying a Bridgestone 350, attention should be paid to all aspects of the bike's condition and care taken to be sure that no parts are missing. These bikes are relatively rare and most replacement parts are difficult to find.

Marusho/Lilac

The company that manufactured both the Marusho and the Lilac motorcycles was started by Masashi Ito in 1948 as the Marusho Shokai Co. Ltd. Between 1948 and 1950, Marusho Shokai developed its first motorcycle, the prototype ML model. The company's first production motorcycle, the LB, a 150 cc single, was manufactured in 1951. Also in 1951, the company name was changed to the Marusho Industrial Motorcycle Company Ltd. Between 1951 and 1959, Marusho made 31 models of Lilacs for the Japanese home market, all but two having shaft drive. It manufactured vertical singles, opposed twins, and scooters. By 1959, the design of Lilac's motorcycles was becoming dated, so a new line of V-twins was developed and put into production.

In 1960 Marusho decided to start exporting bikes to the United States. M-C (Magnera-Clawson) Supply Co. in Los Angeles was chosen as the U.S. importer, and three models of the V-twins were chosen for the U.S. market, the 125 cc CF-40, the 250 cc LS-18, and the 300 cc MF-39. All these bikes shared many significant features, including shaft-drive, two batteries, and a large dyna-starter, which started the engine by directly turning the crankshaft. They all also had several weaknesses, however, including poor-quality pistons and a poor engine lubrication system.

In 1961, motorcycle production stopped due to the company's bankruptcy. When Marusho went bankrupt, M-C Supply's involvement with Lilac ended. During the short period of time that M-C Supply was the Lilac importer, there were reportedly 800 total motorcycles imported.

In 1963, the company was reorganized as the Lilac Co. Ltd., and motorcycle production was restarted in 1964 using the Marusho brand name. Also in 1964, the U.S. Marusho Corp. was formed in California to import the motorcycles into the United States. Starting in 1965 the 500 cc opposed-twin Marusho ST was available in the United States, followed by the Magnum in 1966 and the Electra in 1967. In each of the three years sales declined steadily, with 1967 being the final year for the Marusho. Of the Lilac/Marusho motorcycles imported to the United States, the most significant were the Lilac LS-18 and the Marusho series ST, Magnum and Electra.

1959–1964, LS-18 (247 cc)

Collectibility	★★
Passenger Accommodations	★
Reliability	★★
Parts/Service Availability	★
Handling	★
Engine Performance	★ 1/2

Engine	V-twin cylinder, overhead valve, four-stroke
Bore & stroke	54x54 mm
Displacement	247 cc
Compression ratio	7.8:1
Bhp at rpm	18.5 at 7,800
Transmission	4 speed rotary shift
Primary drive	n/a
Clutch	multi disc, wet plate
Brakes: front	single-leading-shoe drum
Brakes: rear	single-leading-shoe drum
Tire size: front	3.00x17
Tire size: rear	3.25x17
Fuel capacity	2.9 gal
Wheelbase	53 in.
Weight	363 lb
Seat height	28.5 in.
Quarter-mile	n/a
Top Speed	81 mph (approximate)

The LS-18 was manufactured from 1959 through 1964, with only a very few being made during the bankruptcy period of 1962 through 1964. The LS-18 engine was a longitudinally-mounted 90-degree V-twin inspired by the very similar 350 cc Victoria Bergmeister. It used shaft-drive and had a four-speed transmission with a rotary shift pattern, as was seen on some Hondas and Bridgestones of the period. Suspension was the common telescopic front forks and twin shock swingarm rear suspension. The engine was rated at 18.5 horsepower and the claimed top speed was about 80 miles per hour.

Ralph Walker's Lilac MF-39, another version of the Lilac V-twin. This version displaces 288 cc and produces 20 horsepower. The gas tank styling from the MF-39 was used on the later Marusho ST. *Ralph Walker*

A very stylish rear three-quarter view of the Marusho Magnum. *Ralph Walker*

The LS-18 styling was very attractive and other than the V-twin engine, the design of the bike was comparable to many of the other motorcycles being manufactured in Japan during this time. The LS-18s, as previously mentioned, had several weak points, which included a marginal engine lubrication system and pistons prone to seizure.

Today, the LS-18 is more common than either the smaller CF-40 or the larger MF-39. It should be remembered that all Lilacs are rare motorcycles, and although usually reasonably priced, they are seldom seen for sale. Lilac LS-18s are rare bikes and parts are difficult to find. When buying an LS-18, be sure to consider the cost and time to replace any missing or damaged parts.

1965–1967, ST, Magnum, Magnum Electra (493 cc)

Collectibility	★★ 1/2
Passenger Accommodations	★★★
Reliability	★
Parts/Service Availability	★
Handling	★★
Engine Performance	★★

Engine	opposed twin cylinder, overhead valve, four-stroke
Bore & stroke	68x68 mm
Displacement	493 cc
Compression ratio	9.6:1
Bhp at rpm	40 at 7,000 (estimated)
Transmission	5 speed
Primary drive	n/a
Clutch	single disc, dry plate
Brakes: front	single-leading-shoe drum
Brakes: rear	single-leading-shoe drum
Tire size: front	3.25-18
Tire size: rear	3.50-18
Fuel capacity	4.0 gal
Wheelbase	55.0 in.
Weight	406 lb
Seat height	32.0 in.
Quarter-mile	15.7 sec at 84 mph*
Top Speed	96 mph*

Cycle World magazine test, May 1967

Ralph Walker's beautiful Marusho Magnum, showing the bike's very attractive styling. Note the styling of the Magnum gas tank in comparison with the MF-39 gas tank. *Ralph Walker*

The ST and the subsequently improved Magnum and Magnum Electra were produced from 1965 to 1967. All three models had a longitudinally-mounted, 500 cc opposed-twin engine with a four-speed transmission. (Interestingly, there was a yellow third gear indicator light, similar to the fifth gear indicator on the Bridgestone 350s.) Front suspension for the Marushos was telescopic forks and rear suspension was by a twin shock swingarm.

In 1965, imports of the first of the three models the ST began, with approximately 600 motorcycles being brought in during the year. The ST engine was rated at 35.6 horsepower, giving the bike a top speed of 79 miles per hour. The STs were either black and silver or optional candy apple red and looked similar to a /2 BMW with the exception of the telescopic front end and sculptured gas tank, which was taken from the Lilac MF-39. The STs can be distinguished from later models by their silver cylinders, 22-millimeter carburetors, and cast-aluminum right side toolbox.

The STs experienced problems with the ring gears, generators, and the ignition advance mechanism. Because of these problems the dealers and the importer cannibalized many of the bikes for parts. Currently, the Marusho/Lilac Motorcycle Register can account for only 150 of the approximately 600 STs produced.

In 1966 the model name was changed to the Magnum. Magnums were available in black or the optional candy apple red. The compression ratio for the engine was raised and larger carburetors were used, increasing the power output to 40 horsepower. Claimed top speed for the Magnum was 100 miles per hour.

The Magnum can be distinguished by its black cylinders, larger 28 millimeter carburetors, a chromed steel rather than the earlier cast-aluminum right side tool box, and a cheaper throttle cable system. Additionally, gold chevrons appear on the rear fender. Sixty-three of the 180 magnums produced have been accounted for by Marusho/Lilac Motorcycle Register.

In 1967, a new version of the Magnum was introduced as the Magnum Electra. The Electra name reflected the introduction of electric starting for the Magnum. Improvements also included a change from a 6-volt to a 12-volt electrical system, heavier cylinders and a cartridge oil filter system, and a chrome grab bar at the rear of the seat.

The Electra engine was the same as the Magnum with the addition of the electric start. Performance claims were similar to the Magnum, with *Cycle World* recording a top speed of 96 miles per hour in its road test. The Marusho/Lilac Motorcycle Register has accounted for 50 of the 123 Electras built. The final year for Marusho production was 1967.

As can be seen by the number of Marushos that have been accounted for, these are rare motorcycles. If you are looking for an interesting motorcycle that is out of the ordinary, any of the Marushos would be worth the search.

Tohatsu

Tohatsu was founded in October 1922 as the Takata Motor Research Institute. The business was successful and in 1939, the company was renamed the Tokyo Hatsudoki Company Ltd. Prior to World War II, Tokyo Hatsudoki Company Ltd. was a manufacturer of internal combustion engines and, during the war, a supplier of generators to the Japanese armed forces. After World War II, with its main customers gone, the company switched to the manufacture of outboard motors, fire fighting pumps, irrigation pumps, and gasoline engines. In 1950 Tokyo Hatsudoki Company Ltd. began motorcycle production and sales for the Japanese home market under the Tohatsu name.

Here is a view of the Magnum opposed-twin engine showing the similarity to the BMW engine of the time. The Magnum engine was rated at 40 horsepower at 7,000 rpm. *Ralph Walker*

A Tohatsu sales brochure cover promoting the "Push-Button Starters." The motorcycle is a 125 cc LD-3. *Tohatsu*

This is a Runpet Sport 50 CA-2. You can see the "Number Plate" bags and the small windscreen. This particular bike has the home market flat handlebars on it. *Dick Warner*

In the early 1960s, the U.S. importer Hap Jones Distributing Company in San Francisco began bringing Tohatsus into the United States, and by 1962 the Tohatsu sales brochure for the U.S. market showed six models in three displacements. The 50 cc, 60 cc, and one of the 125 cc models were two-stroke air-cooled singles, with the other 125s being two-stroke air-cooled twins. Engine lubrication on all models was by the traditional fuel oil premix method. In addition, several other bikes are shown in the 1962 brochure, a 250 cc two-stroke twin scrambler with a note saying that the model would be available in mid-1962 and a 125 cc two-stroke single scrambler with a handwritten note saying "not available yet." To the best of my knowledge, neither of the scramblers ever became available. A 125 cc race-kit-equipped LD-3 is shown as well as the 50 cc and 125 cc Factory Racing Machines. A note printed below both factory racers states, "Not for sale."

Tohatsu motorcycle production continued until February 1964, when the company claimed bankruptcy. It is reported that after motorcycle production ceased, most of the company's motorcycle engineers went to work for Bridgestone. Today, Tohatsu no longer builds motorcycles but continues as a major manufacturer of outboard motors for boats. If you are fortunate enough to find an LD-3 for sale, be prepared for a long search to locate any parts that are needed to return the bike to original condition.

1961–1964, Runpet Sport CA-2 (49 cc)

Collectibility	★★
Passenger Accommodations	★
Reliability	★★
Parts/Service Availability	★
Handling	★ 1/2
Engine Performance	★

Engine	single cylinder, two-stroke
Bore & stroke	40x39 mm
Displacement	49 cc
Compression ratio	15:1 (claimed)
Bhp at rpm	6.8 at 10,800
Transmission	3 speed
Primary drive	gear
Clutch	single disc, wet plate
Brakes: front	single-leading-shoe drum
Brakes: rear	single-leading-shoe drum
Tire size: front	2.25-22
Tire size: rear	2.25-22
Fuel capacity	1.45 gal
Wheelbase	43.7 in.
Weight	134.2 lb
Seat height	n/a
Quarter-mile	n/a
Top Speed	57.2 mph (claimed)

A Tohatsu Runpet 50 cc "CA-S TYPE Economy size compact motorcycle," according to the sales brochure. Note the enclosed chain guard and a nice long dual seat. This model also had a windscreen, although overall the bike was not quite as sporty as the Sport 50s. *Dick Warner*

トーハツ スポーツ
sport 125

View of an LD-3 from an early 1960s
Tohatsu sales brochure. *Tohatsu*

The 50 cc Runpet Sport was one of the most popular of the Tohatsu line. The engine was a two-stroke single with a stated compression ratio of 15:1 and power output rated at 6.8 horsepower. Starting was by kickstarter, which was somewhat unusual for a Tohatsu, since most models featured electric starting. Performance was quite good, with a top speed of just over 57 miles per hour.

Features on the bike included a single seat with a luggage rack behind it. On each side of the luggage rack were bags that looked like racing number plates displaying the Runpet Sport model name and the marking "No." followed by space to letter in your number. Adding to the sport image of this model was a small windscreen over the headlight. The fuel tank capacity was under a gallon and a half but cruising range was no problem, even with the small tank, due to a fuel consumption rate of over 100 miles per gallon. Runpets, like all Tohatsus, are rare motorcycles and very difficult to find parts for. Keep this in mind when looking at any Tohatsu for possible purchase.

1961–1964, Sport LD3 (124 cc)

Collectibility	★★
Passenger Accommodations	★★
Reliability	★★
Parts/Service Availability	★
Handling	★★
Engine Performance	★ 1/2

Engine	twin cylinder, two-stroke
Bore & stroke	48x43 mm
Displacement	124 cc
Compression ratio	10.8:1
Bhp at rpm	17 at 8,500
Transmission	5 speed
Primary drive	gear
Clutch	multi disc, wet plate
Brakes: front	twin-leading-shoe drum
Brakes: rear	single-leading-shoe drum
Tire size: front	2.50-18
Tire size: rear	2.75-18
Fuel capacity	3.2 gal
Wheelbase	49.6 in.
Weight	253.4 lb
Seat height	n/a
Quarter-mile	n/a
Top Speed	74.6 mph (claimed)

The Sport LD-3 had a two-stroke, twin-cylinder engine, the Tohatsu standard electric starter and, unusual for the time, a five-speed transmission. Magnesium full width hubs were used for both wheels. A top speed of just under 75 miles per hour was claimed for the LD-3.

As previously mentioned, Tohatsu offered a race-kit version of the LD-3 called the Sport 125 cc Road Racer. The race parts included cylinder heads, pistons, carburetors, intake manifold, air cleaners, expansion chambers, total loss ignition system, and a rear sprocket. Also included was a shorter seat with a turned-up tail section and clip-on handlebars. With number plates and the race parts installed, along with the removal of the regular LD-3 front fork spring covers, the Road Racer was an impressive looking bike.

All Tohatsus are very rare motorcycles, with only a handful of people actively collecting them. Even though extremely rare, when Tohatsus are offered for sale they are usually valued approximately the same as one of the more common Hondas of the same displacement.

Tohatsus, like many of the motorcycles in this book, are good examples of why people find classic and vintage Japanese motorcycles fascinating. If you want an interesting challenge, choose any model Tohatsu and attempt to find one. When you find the model you are looking for, buy it and then attempt to find the parts to restore it. What you'll find is that you will have a long search during which you will meet many interesting people, learn many (perhaps trivial, but interesting) facts, and experience a great deal of enjoyment. After all, the search is a large part of the enjoyment of owning any of the classic Japanese motorcycles.

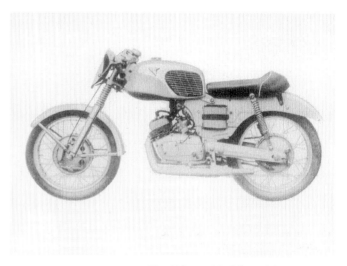

The Tohatsu LD-3 based Sport 125 cc Road Racer with its factory prepped race engine, short seat, modified exhaust system, and many Tohatsu race kit parts. *Tohatsu*

This is a 1964 Trailmaster 50 CA1B with the trail oriented high exhaust and large rear sprocket. A true trail bike of the times. *Jim Elliot*

Appendix

CLUBS AND WEB SITES

The best sources for information, current trends, meet schedules, parts, bikes for sale, online mailing lists and general camaraderie are the clubs dedicated to the collection and preservation of Japanese motorcycles. These range from the all encompassing Vintage Japanese Motorcycle Club to the model specific CBX club to the engine type specific SOHC/4 Owners Club. Many of these clubs have Web sites, which provide information about the club and the particular make or model to which the club is dedicated. In addition, there are also many informative Web sites, some of which have developed into full-fledged clubs and others that have the potential to grow into clubs at some point in the future.

Vintage Japanese Motorcycle Club (VJMC)
VJMC
c/o Ellis Holman
9671 Troon Court
Carmel, IN 46032
http://vjmc.org
> For the owners of all vintage Japanese motorcycles.

SOHC/4 Owners Club
http://www.sohc4.org/main.html
> For the owners of all single overhead cam (SOHC) four-cylinder Hondas.

The International CBX Owners Association (ICOA)
Pete Ruff
ICOA Membership Director
210 Willow Lake Drive
Martinez, CA 94553
http://www.cbxclub.com/
> For Honda CBX owners.

Honda Mini Trail Club: First Kick
1136 Shelterwood
Houston, TX 77008
> For Honda Z50 Mini Trail owners.

Kawasaki Triples Club
1076 N. Gracia
Camarillo, CA 93010
> For owners of Kawasaki three-cylinder two-strokes.

Marusho/Lilac Motorcycle Register
www.geocities.com/MotorCity/Track/2536/index.htm
> For owners of Marusho and Lilac motorcycles.

The Water Buffalo Society, Inc.
3707 South 52nd Street
Milwaukee, WI 53220
http://www.execpc.com/~wtrbuff/society%20page.html
> For owners of Suzuki GTs and RE5s.

Smoke Riders Association
7245 S. 76th Street, Suite 126
Franklin, WI 53132
http://www.execpc.com/~westwind/srmc.html
> Dedicated to two-stroke motorcycles with an emphasis on the Suzuki GT750.

Tohatsu Register
24 Cathy St.
Merrimack, NH 03054
ronbrooksburton@yahoo.com
> For that small group of Tohatsu owners.

XS Eleven Owners Association
http://www.xs11.com/
> For Yamaha XS and XJ1100 owners.

V-Max Owners Association (VMOA)
V.M.O.A.
Attn: Mike Sayers
180 Galilee Rd
Smithfield, NC 27577
http://www.v-max.com/
> For owners of the Yamaha V-Max.

Yamaha 650 Society
P.O. Box 280
Cottleville, MO 63338-0280
http://159.218.3.3/650.htm
> For Yamaha 650 owners.

Turbo Motorcycle International Owners Association (TMIOA)

T.M.I.O.A.
P.O. Box 1653
Albrightsville, PA 18210
www.turbomotorcycles.org
    For the owners of all turbocharged Japanese motorcycles.

The Honda Superhawk Web site
http://www.honda305.com/
    A Web site for the Honda Superhawk

Yamaha TX Interest Site
http://www.delanet.com/~rcole/tx750.htm
    A Web site for the Yamaha TX motorcycles.

Index